ROBERT STEPHEN HAWKER

A Study of His Thought and Poetry

By Margaret F. Burrows, M.A.

Oxford: Basil Blackwell

m cm xxvi

If any Man had written, his Works would best shew to
all intelligent Readers what he was, and that Life or
Delight of the Soul (be it never so Gallant or Glorious)
that is not founded upon deep Humility shall be strongly
shaken with Storms and Tempests . . . .

HENRY MORE.

CONTENTS.

FOREWORD.

THIS study was originally written as a thesis for the degree of M.A. in the University of London. It was felt, however, that the subject was one which might be of interest to a wider circle of readers, and the present publication is the result.

I wish to thank Mr. C. E. Byles, Hawker's son-in-law and chief biographer, and Mrs. Byles, for their generosity in allowing me to use unpublished manuscripts in their possession, and for their helpful advice. I am deeply indebted to Miss Spurgeon, Professor of English Literature in the University of London, to whose inspiration the work is due, and who has given sympathy and encouragement throughout its course. I wish to acknowledge, also, the kindness of Dr. Wilson, Professor of Physics in the same University, in discussing with me certain scientific questions.

M. F. B.

LONDON,
March, 1926.

HAWKER AT THE DOOR OF HIS VICARAGE.

(Taken about 1858.)

INTRODUCTION.

FIFTY years have passed since Robert Stephen Hawker died at Plymouth, his birth-place. The world has forgotten him. Tourists to the north coast of Cornwall learn of him as the eccentric Vicar of Morwenstow ; others have read his " Trelawny Ballad," but know nothing of its author. It is a lean portion indeed, for one who was both poet and mystic, and in justice to him, we must seek the cause of this neglect. We may find an answer in the circumstances of his time.

He led a strangely retired existence. With the exception of six years at Oxford, two later visits there and two to London, his whole life was passed on the borders of Devon and Cornwall. For forty-one years —from 1834 until his death—he was Vicar of Morwenstow, recognised as " a High Churchman " but " by no means an extreme man."[1] On his deathbed, when failing both in body and mind, he was received into the Church of Rome. Fame, who had studiously ignored him all his life, rushed to meet him, though she still had no laurels to offer him. Instead, her chariot wheels bespattered him freely with mud and stones, for was not his act " an unique specimen of treachery to the Church of England ? "[2] Religious feeling in England was in too hysterical a state to consider his, or any such case, dispassionately. The spread of Ritualism ; the reception accorded to the Public Worship Regulation Act ; above all, the claims of Rome, made men fear a repetition of the disasters of " 1844 and 1850 when the most distinguished of our

[1] " Standard," Aug. 18th, 1875.
[2] " John Bull," Sept. 18th, 1875.

ecclesiastics were trooping out of what they held to be a swiftly-falling communion."[1] Public agitation was reflected in the leading articles of the " Times." We are told on September 15th that " more than one of the most civilized nations of the modern days find it necessary to be on their guard against the Pope and his devoted adherents " ; on September 30th we find the statement that " we suspect many a layman has been somewhat startled of late by the pace at which the Clergy run away with the old coach of the Establishment whenever it is repaired "; and on October 19th in a reference to a correspondence on a convert to Rome, we learn that " it appears that the Roman Catholics in this island have achieved one more signal success. One more minute-gun sounds the death of the Establishment and the reign of its successor." The " Morning Post "[2] inserted a paragraph on " Recent Secessions to Rome," of which the last name was that of the Rev. R. S. Hawker, and in spite of letters and articles from friends, the public saw him only as a deserter to Rome, and cared to know no more. Two of his acquaintances, both Church of England clergy, determined to set him right with the world.

The first to finish the task was the Rev. S. Baring-Gould, who published " The Vicar of Morwenstow, being a Life of Robert Stephen Hawker, M.A." in 1876. His aim was to give a picture of the man as he lived and worked among his parishioners, and he was in many ways well-fitted to be Hawker's biographer. He had imagination and sympathy and a facile pen. But his book has one fatal defect—the author is thinking more of himself than of his subject. He wants the book to sell ; he therefore emphasizes those characteristics in Hawker which will attract popular attention, does not scruple to add picturesque details, which have their source only in his imagination, and finally, in order to forestall his rival, hurries

1 " Church Times," Oct. 15th, 1875.
2 Oct. 9th, 1875.

his romantic presentation of Hawker out into the world, a little inaccurate and rather slip-shod. From his point of view the book must have been a success, for it is now in its seventh edition, but he let most of the inaccuracies remain, and it is due to him that Hawker the poet and mystic is still eclipsed by Hawker the parson and eccentric.

His rival, Dr. F. G. Lee, with fewer gifts, was a more conscientious workman, but a partisan. As such, his purpose in writing the " Memorials of the Rev. R. S. Hawker," was two-fold, and his view of Hawker limited. In his own words he wished " to do justice to a venerated priest, who, having been called home, cannot now speak for himself ; and secondly, to warn our ecclesiastical rulers how dangerous is their policy, which has made a non-Christian Parliament, representing Public Opinion, and a Lay-Judge created for the purpose, the interpreter for the National Church, of the Will, the Revelation, and the mode of worship of Almighty God." [1] Mr. Baring-Gould's picture of Hawker may be a caricature, but we can recognize the man ; in Dr. Lee's hands we have but a distorted shadow. He tells us that Hawker was " a Tory by birth and conviction—a respectful admirer of More and Fisher, the noble Laud, the saintly Charles, and the high-principled Sancroft ; a hearty detester of both the Cromwells, all the German reformers, but more especially of William of Orange, Tillotson and Burnet," [2] and this high-handed summary of his theological and political views is matched by the description of his place as a poet. Dr. Lee closes his account of Hawker's " Literary Labours " thus. " As a Christian poet, he will surely be ranked amongst the foremost of the present century, a century which has produced a Wordsworth, a Keble, a Faber, a Neale, an Isaac Williams, and a Miss Procter ! " [3] The real

[1] " Memorials," 1876, p. 201.
[2] Ibid., p. 5.
[3] Ibid., p. 113.

Hawker was now buried even deeper than he had been by Mr. Baring-Gould.

During the next twenty-five years he remained hidden. Two editions of his poems[1] and one of his prose works[2] were issued by the piety of friends, but they seem to have crept into the world unheeded, and though Mr. J. A. Noble, writing an essay on Hawker's poetry, in 1892 declared that "since his death the little group of lovers has grown into a crowd,"[3] it must have been a crowd that dissolved rather than increased. Not until his centenary was Hawker brought to the light. In 1903 his son-in-law, Mr. C. E. Byles, published a new edition of his prose[4] and in 1904 of his poetry.[5] A few journalists read Mr. Baring-Gould's book and wrote humorous articles[6] on an eccentric and an oddity, and then in 1905 Mr. Byles published in his " Life and Letters of R. S. Hawker," a comprehensive and faithful portrait of a fascinating personality. Without that book this study could never have been written, for the letters which it contains reveal unsuspected depths in Hawker's character, and throw light on much that was obscure and confused. They show what lay at the root of all his life—the fact that he was a mystic, and without that knowledge it is impossible to understand him. They show that his thoughts were more important than his deeds, that for him as truly as for Blake, " Thought is Act." Yet the impression left after reading any one of Hawker's biographies is that he was first and foremost a man of action—a busy parish priest, an energetic rescuer of ship-wrecked men, and we overlook the fact that these activities can have taken but little time from the long hours of thought during his secluded

---

[1] Poetical Works, edited J. G. Godwin, 1879.   Poetical Works, edited A. Wallis, 1899.

[2] Prose Works, edited J. G. Godwin, 1893.

[3] " Hawker of Morwenstow," in " The Sonnet in England and other Essays," 1893, p. 182.

[4] " Footprints of Former Men in Far Cornwall."

[5] " Cornish Ballads and other Poems."

[6] Treasury, Dec. 1903. Macmillan's Magazine, Dec. 1904

life at Morwenstow. The extracts from his note-books, published in 1922 under the title, " Stones Broken from the Rocks," give further glimpses into his mind.

It must surely be worth while to throw light on his figure from a different angle, for, though all have allowed him to be a poet, none have considered the poems as part of the man's expression of himself—of as much importance as his actions. They assume an even higher value when we realise that he was a poet who deliberately chose another path, and that apart from them we know very little of the man before he reaches middle age. Though it was inevitable from the ordering of his life that the Vicar should appear more important than the poet, one picture of him is incomplete without the other superimposed upon it, and by his writings he will live when his parish work is forgotten. This study is an attempt to rescue him from the one-sided notoriety, which, in spite of Mr. Byles's portrait, is all he seems to have been accorded, and to present him in such a light that he may after many days be granted the fame which he so earnestly desired during his life.

CHAPTER I.

1803—1846. LIFE AND CHARACTER.

"MY Mother's Father was a Dane . . . . My Ancestor on the Male side came over from Ireland, a Celt and Master of the Hawks to one of the Thomonds—hence the name."[1] Much of Hawker's temperament is explained by this ancestry, for whether the legendary retainer of the Thomonds ever existed apart from his own imagination or not, there is no doubt of the Celtic strain in his blood. To this he owes his love of stormy seas and rugged hills, and by this he shares with Vaughan and Traherne a vivid consciousness of forces not of this world. His imagination is the great Celtic heritage, and its gift, also, the melancholy which attends the dreamer when he leaves the hill-tops of vision for the valley of disillusion. As for that other outstanding characteristic, love of the past — was not a boundless enthusiasm for " former men " and their deeds fitting in one sprung from two races whose fame to-day is but the shadow of their earlier greatness ?

These, however, are all marks of the man whose delight is in contemplation ; we must seek as well the source of those qualities which made him in his own day more conspicuous for his active work as Vicar of Morwenstow than for his thoughts. We have not far to go, for his immediate ancestors were men of practical ability with strong humanitarian instincts, taking for their vocations the cure of either bodies or souls. His great-grandfather was a certain Jacob Hawker, surgeon, Mayor of Exeter in 1744, his grandfather was

[1] " Life and Letters," p. 558.

A

Dr. Robert Hawker, Vicar of Charles Church, Plymouth, from 1784 to 1827, and a famous Calvinistic preacher, and his father, though first a doctor, left this profession for the Church.

Hawker tells us little of his father or grandfather, except that from them he inherited a highly-sensitive nervous system ; " a thought," he writes, " will often stab me like a sword and a Fear or dread will thrill throughout my bodily frame as if some one had struck me a blow."[1] But we cannot lightly dismiss the learned doctor, for, in addition to any qualities he may have handed down to his grandson, he undoubtedly helped to mould his character. All Hawker's early life was spent at Plymouth ; he was born there on December 3rd, 1803, and, when his father went to his first curacy, was left behind in his grandfather's charge. It seems probable that the intense love of the Catholic Church, so marked in Hawker when he reached manhood, was in some measure due to reaction against the severe Calvinism of his early teaching, and it is interesting to note that one to whom Hawker was closely akin in attitude of mind, the Cambridge Platonist, Henry More, had the same experience in his youth.[2] Its effect on Hawker may be seen from a letter of 1857 in which he speaks of the sect of the Plymouth Brethren : " They are usually bitter and furious Calvinists and have been to me all my life a theme of horror. I knew them all too well in my Grandfather's family, and I never recall what I heard and saw among them without a shudder . . . The language you repeat . . . about God's curse and a " Child of the Evil One " is as familiar to my memory as household words and it sounded like the echo of old accustomed phrases to me.[3] The Calvinistic doctrine of " Original Sin," which coloured Hawker's later views on Baptism, was a relic of his early teaching, but as a boy he fortunately

[1] " Life and Letters," p. 524.
[2] Poems of Dr. H. More, edited Grosart, 1878, Introd., p. xii.
[3] " Life and Letters," p. 295.

possessed too much robust vitality to become morbid from it, and a love of practical joking, which remained with him all his life, counteracted any tendency to excessive piety.   Only one of the many anecdotes of his pranks shows the boy's relations with his grandfather, but it is most characteristic. He is said to have made an early attempt at versification by re-writing Dr. Hawker's version of the hymn, " Lord, dismiss us with thy blessing," and to have asked his grandfather if he did not consider the revision an improvement ! In later life Hawker was generally satisfied with his own literary achievement.

One other glimpse into his early life is given by Hawker himself. In an unpublished notebook dated 1857, under the heading, " The Child is Father of the Man," he writes, " I look back and discern my Ancestor, a shrinking apprehensive boy, clad in clouted clothes, hurrying through the streets away from the scorn of other boys, crouching among the pledges in a Pawnbroker's Warehouse in a reeky Plymouth Street to devour the Arabian Nights and with an Imagery of Mind even then creative clothing that foul den with forms of Fancy's Mould until that Southside Street Shop became the palace of Aladdin's Lamp." The mind of the solitary child must have been wellnigh starved for lack of imaginative literature in his grandfather's severe household.

After attending various preparatory schools, from which he ran away in turn, as he hated restraint of any kind, he consented to stay at the Grammar School at Liskeard, and spent his holidays at his own home, as his father had now become Curate of Stratton. His friend of later years, Mr. Maskell, tells us that " as a boy he was indulged by his parents, and seems to have been by no means easy to control."[1] He certainly took little interest in his school tasks, as we know from his own admission, and his brain found more congenial work in planning original ways of amusing or annoy-

[1] Pamphlet embodying reviews from the Athenæum, 1876, p. 6

ing the good people of Stratton. Too much emphasis
has been laid on these schoolboy pranks in earlier biographies, but though they need not be described at
length, they must not be wholly ignored, for Hawker's
love of hoaxing stayed with him all his life. Moreover,
two of these practical jokes reveal so clearly the per-
petrator's eye for artistic effect that they are too
illuminating to omit. On one occasion Hawker trans-
formed the appearance of the doctor's horse by cutting
short its mane and painting its body with stripes of
black paint. In order that this work of art should be
seen of all, he sent an urgent message that the doctor
was needed to attend a patient some miles away, and
he, having no other means of conveyance, had to ride
his extraordinary-looking animal right through the
town, only to find on arrival at his destination that no
message had been sent.   In the other prank, Hawker
is not only stage-manager, but leading actor as well,
for a joke, well-remembered in that district, was his
dramatic representation of a mermaid. Choosing a
moonlight night, he took up his position on one of the
rocks near Bude, draped himself with sea-weed, and
by combing his hair and singing, successfully deceived
many of the country folk, until a farmer brought his
performance to an end by trying to shoot him.

His parents, although indulgent of his mischievous
ways, were probably prevented by lack of means from
letting him follow his own inclination in the choice of
a profession, for after leaving school he was given work
by a friend of the family, a solicitor at Plymouth.
There is no scope for imaginative work in the study of
law, and it is not surprising that Hawker soon left it.
Fortunately, money for his further education was now
available, for his aunt, Mrs. Hodson, offered to pay
his expenses at Cheltenham Grammar School. It was
about two years later—in 1821—that he issued a
document of the greatest interest to students of his
character—his first book of poems, " Tendrils," by
" Reuben."

With the publication of this we have an opportunity of gaining first-hand information of what was passing through the mind of the eighteen-year-old boy. We already know that he possessed a most active imagination to which he had given play in practical jokes planned with a due consideration for artistic effect. It is only natural that he should turn to verse as a means of expression—many boys of less mental energy than himself have chosen the same. Hawker's little book is far more worthy of study than one would gather from the contemptuous criticism pronounced on it by Mr. J. Ashcroft Noble in 1892. In his essay on Hawker's poetry, he writes : — " The booklet was not remarkable in any way, and not even interesting save as another illustration of the fact that even in the work of unmistakeably original poets imitativeness precedes originality."[1] We are not concerned here with the literary merits of the volume, but the inaccuracy of the further statement " that there is nothing to be learned of the inner life of those ' prentice days ' "[2] has already been pointed out by Mr. Byles, who comments on the author's love of nature, and interest in legend and superstition,[3] and there is still more to be gleaned by a closer search.

At the outset we are met by a preface, which it will be convenient to discuss according to its position in the printed volume rather than its date of composition. For several reasons it demands quotation. It has not been printed since Mr. Godwin's edition of the Poetical Works in 1879, and those critics who have read it have seen in it the most opposite characteristics. It runs as follows :—" When a first attempt is submitted to public notice and judgment, its readers may very naturally desire to know somewhat concerning him who has the temerity to make it.

" But the writer of the following rhymes has little

[1] " The Sonnet in England," p. 184.
[2] *Ibid.*, p. 187.
[3] " Life and Letters," p. 10.

in himself to excite interest and less to afford gratification ; he is content to wrap the veil of obscurity around his head until the voice of public opinion shall have passed by.

" To apologise in some measure, however, for the abundant imperfections of the first effort of his pen, he would express a hope that the productions of one over whom eighteen summers have scarcely passed will carry some excuse with them ; and as his motive for thrusting them on the world, he would plead that a measure of vanity is meted to us all, and his portion has been in no wise withheld." Does this piece of fine writing show, as Mr. Byles thinks, " a modesty and candour all too infrequent among youthful poets,' or is it, as the writer of the essay in Macmillan's Magazine for December, 1904, suggests, an acknowledgement of a weakness which was to characterise Hawker throughout his life ? It will be only too clear that the latter interpretation is the true one ; vanity was Hawker's besetting sin.

The poems themselves are unequal in quality, and probably their composition extended over a period of at least two years. Perhaps " The Fairy Vision," with its close imitation of " Lalla Rookh," was written before he left Stratton, and the poems dealing with his home were evidently composed soon after his first departure from it. As poetry they have no value, but Hawker so seldom speaks of his early life that we seize eagerly on these fragments. He has the same clinging affection for the security of home that the youth Tennyson had.

> I have been a young pilgrim from the place
> Which holds my all of love : and tho' my staff
> Of wandering is but green, I love to think
> Upon the hour when my warm heart shall hail
> Its vanished home once more.[1]

And these lines reveal not only boyish homesickness, but one of the underlying traits of Hawker's charac-

[1] " Cornish Ballads," 1908, p. 250.

ter—an almost primitive passion for his home. An event at school is commemorated in " Introductory and Farewell Verses intended to be recited at a public examination," and some of the later poems seem to have been written during the holidays, one being definitely dated as " Written on Efford Down Cliff in the autumn of 1820." Efford was the home of the daughters of Colonel Wrey I'ans, one of whom probably inspired the poem, " A Remembrance."

More important, however, than the record of these minor events are the themes which interest the poet. In the verses entitled " What Lovest Thou ? " he has given a list of the objects of his enthusiasm, and for this reason the verses may be quoted in spite of their lack of originality and faulty workmanship.

> I love the song of tender feeling
>   Fair lips begin :
> I love soft eyes of light, revealing
>   The soul within.
>
> I love the lark of summer, winging
>   Its song-cheered way ;
> And dear to me the mavis, singing
>   Her evening lay.
>
> Sweet is the violet returning
>   To starlit sleep ;
> And fair the rosebud of the morning
>   Where dewdrops weep.
>
> I seek the stream of gentle flowing
>   Where suns are bright ;
> And hail the chastened moon bestowing
>   Her silver light.
>
> I trace the shades of sunset, fleeting
>   O'er the blue tide ;
> And dancing waves the day-beam meeting
>   As if in pride.
>
> I seek the spot where fairies dancing
>   Have traced their path
> (When midnight stars are brightly glancing)
>   To tempt their wrath.

> Lady, there's not a light ray streaming
>   From skies above,
> On earth there's not a flow'ret beaming
>   I do not love.[1]

A " sentimental journey," indeed, and if the volume contained nothing more, Mr. Noble's criticism would have been just, though he might have made allowances for Hawker, if he had taken into account the low level to which poetry had sunk at that time. An age which could acclaim Mrs. Hemans as a great poetess was easily satisfied—indeed, it preferred sentiment watered down and well sugared. Hawker might still have developed into a great poet if all his *juvenilia* had been mawkish and artificial, for these are no worse than some of Tennyson's first poems, but there are signs in the volume of a more virile side to his character. Though there are callow imitations of Moore, such as the lament for the lost " Rose of the Valley," and his love of the sea is described in lines after the manner of Byron, he has chosen worthier leaders than these. Drawing inspiration from the Bible, he visualises the scenes of Jewish history in a paraphrase of David's Lament over Jonathan, and in Deborah's Song of Victory ; and with Scott before him, writes a tribute to a lost leader and mourns the fall of a disgraced chieftain, thus expressing for the first time an interest in the past which was to become one of the chief motives of his work. This serious note is struck again in some of the poems on nature, for they contain, beside rhapsodies on the beauty of land and sea, day and night, such lines on the passing of life and love, as these :

> Learn thou that friendship passeth as the wind,
> That love will fade, and trust thou not in man ![2]

Even more significant as heralds of his later sense of " the present calling to the past " are two couplets in the poem, " Nature."

---

[1] " Cornish Ballads," 1908, p. 274.
[2] *Ibid.*, p. 271.

Where chieftains dwelt the ivy-wreaths have grown,
And foxes earth'd beneath the sculptured stone,
Where goblets circled and where minstrels sung,
The midnight bird is nestling o'er her young.[1]

Interesting, too, is the metaphor of the vine, worked out in the opening " Sonnet "—so-called—from which the volume takes its name, in view of the poet's later love of symbolism and use of the same picture to teach " a parable divine."

As one would expect, the author gained little from his book except the satisfaction of seeing his poems in print, and, though a note many years after bears witness to " disappointment in literary undertakings, cf. Cheltenham, 1820,"[2] in his old age he had forgotten even the title of the volume. In 1871 he wrote to a friend, " I have but a hazy recollection of the Cheltenham affair. ' Fibres ' is the nearest guess I can make," and later, " If ' Fibres ' fail, why not try ' Pendicles '? " Just in passing, one wonders whether Hawker suggested this in all seriousness, or whether in his old age he was conscious that as a boy he lacked the saving grace of humour.

Hawker left Cheltenham in 1823, and spent the next six years at Oxford. For the first year he was a student of Pembroke, but after his marriage at the end of 1823 had to move to Magdalen Hall. According to official records he won the Newdigate Prize in 1827, took his B.A. in 1828, and, having subsequently read for Orders, was ordained Deacon in 1829. Between the lines of this bald statement of facts we may read much. Change of environment alone must have deeply affected one so sensitive to his surroundings as Hawker. After the rugged beauty of the Cornish coast, the quiet country-side of Oxford had as little appeal for him as that of Cambridge for Wordsworth, but the city itself with its enshrined memories of the past took a firm hold on his imagination and affections. He refers

[1] " Cornish Ballads," 1908, p. 270.
[2] " Life and Letters," p. 11.

to Oxford as " the only place out of my own house that I ever cared to see."[1] He now had all the resources of the Bodleian to satisfy that hunger for books, which his friend, Mr. Christopher Harris, noted as a characteristic of his youth. Writing of the daughters of Colonel I'ans, one of whom became Hawker's wife, he says : " In the society of these ladies, at Bude, Hawker spent most of his time. Young, handsome and brilliant, he was ever a welcome guest. His craving after knowledge was notorious. Books such as he desired were not to be found at Stratton ; and the library at Whitstone, small yet well selected, furnished the means of gratification."[2] Hawker's own letters in later life show the delight which he felt at having access to an unlimited number of books. In 1857 he writes, " I sometimes think that I have exhausted the usual interests of a literary life by having read so greedily in early life. Not that I pretend to be a learned man beyond my fellows, but from reading very fast, especially at Oxford, I have gone through a vast Number of Books."[3] It was through the medium of books that Hawker's mental outlook was widened, rather than through contact with other minds.

Yet a man of keen intelligence, however original his own mind is, cannot be unaffected by those most intimate with him. Early in his University career, Hawker married Miss Charlotte I'ans, a lady twenty years older than himself. He had known her from his childhood, and they had tastes in common, surely sufficient grounds for explaining the marriage without suggesting, as Mr. Baring-Gould does,[4] that Hawker had an eye on her annuity of £200 a year. Certainly her money came in very useful at various times, as we shall see, but we feel assured that Hawker's love for her was never tainted by any sordid motive. For forty years of his life she is a shadowy figure in the back-

[1] " Life and Letters," p. 18.
[2] " John Bull," April 15th, 1876, quoted in " Life and Letters," p. 16.
[3] " Life and Letters," p. 297.
[4] " Vicar of Morwenstow," 1919, p. 15.

ground, and, except for his references to her care and devotion, our knowledge of her is confined to Mr. Maskell's description of her as " a person of considerable attractions, well-educated, fond of literature, a good companion and in every respect a lady." We may see her influence in the translations of some of Goethe's and Schiller's poems which Hawker made in 1826, for she herself translated stories from German literature.

In friendships with fellow-students Hawker probably gave more than he received. According to Dr. Lee, " he was known to a wide circle of friends for his frankness of manner, sweetness of temper, ready wit, accurate scholarship, general literary ability and remarkable powers of conversation."[1] No doubt his readiness to enter into a practical joke made him a popular figure, but his real character can be seen in his choice of intimate friends. Mr. Byles records that " at Pembroke he had made the acquaintance of Francis Jeune, afterwards Bishop of Peterborough. Other friends were William Jacobson, of Lincoln College, afterwards Bishop of Chester, and Arthur Kelly of Kelly in Devon, then at Corpus, and Sir Thomas Acland at Christ Church,"[2] Of these, the latter can hardly be considered a college friend, for he was sixteen years older than Hawker, and had left Oxford many years before. With Arthur Kelly, later Sheriff of Cornwall, the bond was probably one of interest in the same locality ; both were natives of the western land, sensitive to its beauty, and Hawker printed in his 1836 volume verses by Mr. Kelly, with the note, " I insert them here partly from their extreme beauty ; partly because they express thoughts congenial with my own, and partly as a memorial of collegiate friendship between the author and myself kept hitherto ' unspotted by the world '."

Still closer was the relation between Hawker and the two future bishops. He himself writes, " In 1825

1 " Memorials," p. 3.
2 " Life and Letters," p. 17.

three men in Oxford formed a friendship. They studied, read, walked and talked together from that date for three years there."[1] Dean Burgon, in his essay on Jacobson, expresses surprise at this friendship, for " that eccentric individual, the Rev. Robert S. Hawker of Morwenstow, *seemed* Jacobson's very opposite. There was a considerable bond between them notwithstanding ; how cemented I know not."[2] Burgon, however, was mistaken in thinking that Hawker was Jacobson's pupil, when the latter became Vice-Principal of Magdalen Hall in 1832, and no doubt we may assume that Jeune, with whom Hawker made that hilarious " Ride from Bude to Boss," described in " Footprints of Former Men in Far Cornwall," formed the connecting link. But the very fact that Hawker was on such terms with an undergraduate, " endowed with excellent abilities, a resolute will, great strength and steadfastness of purpose, fired also . . . by a holy ambition and animated by the loftiest principle,"[3] in addition to which, according to one of his own letters, he was " looked on in College as a sort of oracle in the way of Divinity,"[4] proves the existence of a serious and thoughtful mind hidden under Hawker's jovial manner. It is upheld, too, by other friendships referred to only by Hawker, who writes of the Wilberforces, " I was at Oxford with two of them, Robert and Samuel, and they were both friends of mine. I always thought Robert the highest intellect, and no man was ever more esteemed and respected by another than I myself was by Robert W."[5]

Mr. Byles thinks that " although the Tractarian movement had begun to stir the mind of Oxford in his undergraduate days, he left the University too early to be much concerned in it . . . His innate love of

[1] " Life and Letters," p. 17.
[2] Burgon, " Twelve Good Men," ed. 1891, p. 385.
[3] *Ibid.*, p. 369.
[4] *Ibid.*, p. 370.
[5] " Life and Letters," p. 304.

symbolism and intense reverence for the past were enough of themselves to shape his course."[1] Yet with four friends who were later to hold high positions in the Church; with " Newman, Pusey, Ward, Marriott . . . all in the common room every evening discussing, talking, reading,"[2] as he writes reminiscently in 1861, he cannot have been unaffected by the ideas which were leavening the thought of Oxford. One would like to imagine that the " wonderful scholar, theologian and Tory, Martin Joseph Routh (1755—1854), President of Magdalen, reserved, as Newman wrote in 1838, ' to report to a forgetful generation what was the theology of their fathers,' "[3] had indirectly influenced a simple undergraduate, who was in his turn to excite his teacher's imagination by his writings. The President's recitation of " a quatrain relating to the threatened fate of one of the seven deprived bishops " was so characteristic that Dean Burgon thought it worth while to give details of the emphasis and actions in each line of the verse :

> And shall Trelawny die ?
> And shall Trelawny die ?
> Here's twenty thousand Cornish men
> Will know the reason why ![4]

With this step we reach well-trodden ground— Hawker's most popular poem, " The Song of the Western Men," or " Trelawny Ballad." Taking the old chorus quoted above, which has been " ever since the imprisonment by James the Second of the seven bishops . . . a popular proverb throughout Cornwall," he built round it a poem, which throughout its existence has drawn attention to itself, while others of his writings of far greater interest have been neglected. Composed during a vacation of 1824, it was first published anonymously in a Plymouth paper. Its later adventures are described by Hawker in a letter of

[1] "Life and Letters," p. 121.
[2] *Ibid.*, p. 19.
[3] Camb. Hist., vol. XII., ch. xii., p. 260.
[4] Burgon, " Twelve Good Men," ed. 1891, p. 34.

1862. " Everybody liked it. *It*, not myself, became popular. I was unnoted and unknown. It was seen by Mr. Davies Gilbert, President of the Society of Antiquaries, etc., etc., and by him reprinted at his own Private Press at Eastbourne. Then it attracted the notice of Sir Walter Scott, who praised it, not me, unconscious of the Author. Afterwards Macaulay (Lord) extolled it in his ' History of England,' and again Dickens in ' Household Words.' All these years the Song has been bought and sold, set to music and applauded."[1] Again we see fatal vanity peeping out, and the history of the poem seems a judgment on it. From its inclusion in the various anthologies it is probably the only poem by which Hawker is known to-day, and still it is the poem, and not the author, which is appreciated. Whatever the causes of this popularity, its chief interest for us at this point is that it shows Hawker turning to the past for his theme, while the only other poem of this time, " Clovelly," is inspired by the beauty of nature ; and thus these poems are representative of the two trains of thought which run side by side through his work. The third poem of these years, " Pompeii," may be disregarded, for, as it was written in competition for the Newdigate Prize, its subject was not Hawker's own choice.

In 1829, Hawker, now a Deacon, was appointed to the curacy of N. Tamerton, near Whitstone, and so was once more resident in his own beloved county. In 1831 he was ordained priest, and the next year published a small volume of poems under the title, " Records of the Western Shore." Of the fourteen new poems, the majority, according to dates in Mr. Godwin's edition, were written in 1831 or 1832. Probably at first the work of his parish took most of his time, for from a letter of 1858 we learn that he had gained many of the threads for the material of the ballads on his vacation tour to " Boscastle, Tintagel and the Cornish Moorlands in that District." He continues,

---

[1] " Life and Letters," p. 23.

" My custom of turning things into rhyme had received encouragement in the University by the Newdigate Prize for ' Pompeii,' which I had won in 1827. In the course of our tour whatsoever germs of legend or tale came in my way, I forthwith put into verse and among others as I confess, on very slight ground of local suggestion, I did invent the Ballad that I enclose." This was " The Silent Tower of Bottreaux," the most interesting of the ballads in the volume, for the others, although not without a value of their own, have nothing in them which marks them as unmistakeably Hawker's. On the other hand, in " The Silent Tower," the story is original ; " the sole materials," he tells us, " that I gathered on the spot were that a certain Church Tower on the sea-shore, called in reality Forrabury, but by myself in poetic licence, Bottreaux, was devoid of Bells."[1] Above all, Hawker is dealing with subjects very dear to him—religion and nature.

We must turn to another poem in the volume to find out what each meant to him. At first sight it is a fragment as rugged as the scene it describes, and probably as such was excluded from Mr. Godwin's collection, but a closer view shows it to be a full circle of thought struck out in strange rhythmic lines. " A Rapture on the Cornish Hills," as he calls it, no doubt intending the full meaning to be read into the word, is the story of an experience of the soul. Its value is as that of a diamond among stones of little worth.

> I stood at the foot of Rocky Carradon—
> The massive monuments of a vast religion,
> Piled by the strength of unknown hands, were there.
> The everlasting hills, around, afar,
> Uplifted their huge fronts, the natural altars
> Reared by the Earth to the surrounding God.
> I heard a Voice, as the sound of many waters :—
> " What do'st thou here, Elijah ? " And I said,
> " What doth *he* here, Man that is born of woman ?
> The clouds may haunt these mountains ; the fierce storm

---

[1] " Life and Letters," p. 262.

Coiled in his caverned lair—that wild torrent
Leaps from a native land ; but Man ! O Lord !
What doth *he* here ? '

Stranger.   Did'st thou not fear the Voice ?
The Bard.   I could not, at the foot of rocky Carradon.[1]

Before this poem Hawker has given no expression to
" the deep things " of the soul. With no diary, no sub-
jective poetry to help us, we have been walking in the
dark, and probably misled by wandering lights. The
stories of his exuberant physical energy make it easy
for us to overlook the serious side of his character,
and, even if it is noticed, there have been no signs of
great spiritual vitality.   The fact that he has taken
Orders does not in itself prove the existence of this.
With grandfather and father both in the Church, he
might have followed in their steps as a matter of
family tradition.   It was not so long since Sydney
Smith, following his father's wishes, had taken it up
as his profession instead of the law for which he was
so well fitted. But this record of spiritual experience
shows us that Hawker was a poet with the outlook of
a mystic, and in that lies the key to his whole life.
How far he journeys on the Mystic Way, what hills of
difficulty and sloughs of despond in turn hinder his
progress, will appear as we trace his steps ; this poem
shows that he has the distinguishing mark of the true
mystic—he has lived through the unforgettable moment in which a vision of Reality was vouchsafed to
the expectant soul.

The setting is " the hilly moorland stretching from
Rough Tor to Carradon " near a " cromlech, piled
rocks, and unhewn pillar "—relics of some ancient
worship. As he meditates on the attributes of God,
which these suggest—His eternal glory, worshipped
by generations of men, His unchanging might, declared by the natural world with its strength in hills
and storms—the veil of time and space is rent away.
Words, addressed first to a prophet of old, later an

---

[1] " Cornish Ballads," 1908, p. 38.

inspiration to a mystic, like Hawker steeped in the lore of the Old Testament,[1] bring the poet into conscious relation with the Divine—the God, in Whom " we live and move and have our being." Faced with the values of eternity, the soul must adjust itself to this higher plane. It is convinced of its own high destiny, for the words, " Come to thy God in time . . . . Come to thy God at last," in " The Silent Tower of Bottreaux," speak of its consummation, and so, without semblance of fear, seeks to know the meaning of its life in this world of matter—" What doth he here, Man that is born of Woman ? " An unanswered question—yes, but the mystic, in spite of doubts, knows what he should do. The answer for Hawker is given in his own words many years later (1860). " What, I wonder, was the purpose of my life ? . . . All was done for the wisest and the best ; of this be very sure. But still, I wonder why—O may God grant that I may have bound up the wounds of at least one by the wayside ! that I may have carried a cup of cold water in these hands to *one for whom Christ died*. If I have been his Vicar, but to one of his lowly ones, I shall not have lived in vain."[2]

The form, then, that Hawker's mysticism takes is " in essence, the concentration of all the forces of the soul upon a Supernatural Object, conceived and loved as a Living Person."[3] Love demands a life of service and self-sacrifice ; the artist in him, in so far as self-expression is a form of egotism, must take second place. The truth of this is clear from the Preface to this volume, in which he says, " The simple legends . . . were ' done into verse ' . . . during these my walks and rides, and this I mention ' lest an enemy should say ' that I had borrowed for this purpose any of the time belonging to the graver duties of a severe profession. I could indeed have wished to have ' grappled

[1] *Cf.* Blake, " Vision of the Death of Abel."
[2] " Life and Letters," p. 327.
[3] Berger, " William Blake," p. 72, quoted by E. Underhill, " Mysticism," p. 106.

B

with a loftier theme,' but the cares and duties of a
busy life forbid me to indulge this hope." Unlike
George Herbert, who determined to be first a good
poet, and afterwards a good priest, Hawker considers
his literary work a form of self-indulgence,—as indeed
in these early poems, it is. Vanity is his greatest weakness, and at present he is writing, not because he must,
but with an eye to fame. In the dedication he is quite
frank about it.

> What is my wish ?   Not that an echoing crowd
> Publish my praises on some distant strand ;
> Not that the voices of those men be loud
> With whom a strange and nameless man I stand :
> 'Tis the fond vision that some western hand
> Will turn this page—a native lip proclaim
> Him who lov'd well and long the Rocky Land.
> Hills of Old Cornwall ! in your antique fame
> Oh ! that a voice unborn might blend my future name !

As the years pass, this desire for personal glory will be
commuted to something less ignoble, but when he
realises that his gift of song may also be dedicated to
the service of God, various difficulties combine to
hinder composition. Thus it is to Hawker's mysticism
that we must look for an explanation of his compara-
tively small literary output.

Four years elapsed before another volume of poems
was published. In 1834 Hawker became Vicar of the
parish of Morwenstow, where he was to work for the
rest of his life.   His duties there needed all his energy,
for there was much to be done in both mundane and
spiritual matters. He writes later, " When I was col-
lated in 1834 to this Living by the Bishop, it was with
the stipulation, ' You will have to build a new house
on the Glebe, Mr. H.,' " and a letter of 1856 gives
further details. " Full of hope and burning with zeal,
I was about to accomplish great things. My parish
(the Methodist Preachers were so prosperous here that
one of them told me on my arrival that Morwenstow
was the Garden of their Circuit)—my Parish, I say,

was to become a model on the Cornish coast."[1] It is
not surprising, therefore, that the second series of
" Records of the Western Shore," published in 1836,
contained only thirteen new poems, excluding " The
Wreck," which Hawker later declared to be his wife's
composition.

Small as it is, the volume is not lacking in interest.
Though the poet is not unconcerned with the opinions
of his readers, for he prefixes the quotation from
Milton, " Fit audience find, though few," he has made
no attempt to catch the popular ear, and his motive is
altruistic—he wishes to earn money for the re-build-
ing of the Parochial School.   But he is still much interested in himself, and poem after poem speaks of the
conflict raging in his soul. In the opening poem,
" Cornwall," later entitled " The Western Shore," he
unburdens his heart.

> Thou lovely land ! where, kindling, throng
> Scenes that should breathe the soul of song :
> Home of high hopes that once were mine
> Of loftier verse and nobler line !
>
> 'Tis past—the quenched volcano's tide
> Sleeps well within the mountain side :
> Henceforth shall time's cold touch control
> The warring Hecla of my soul.
>
> Welcome ! wild rock and lonely shore,
> Where round my days dark seas shall roar ;
> And this gray fane, Morwenna, stand
> The beacon of the Eternal Land ! [2]

The struggle is not easily won.   Even a poem inspired
by the " gray fane," Minster Church, and the service
of Confirmation opens with a half-hearted repudiation
of fame.

> ang not the harp upon the willow-bough,
> But teach thy native echoes one more song,
> Though fame withhold her sigil from thy brow,

[1] " Life and Letters," p. 75.
[2] " Cornish Ballads." 1908, p. 56.

B 2

And years half yield thee to the unnoted throng.
Doth not the linnet her meek lay prolong
In the lone depths of some deserted wood ?
Springs not the violet coarse weeds among
Where no fond voice shall praise her solitude ?
Happy that bird and flower, though there be few intrude ! [1]

Yet this is not enough to account for the sadness which is the key-note of the whole volume. As poet, Hawker has to cast selfish ambition from him, but as man and as priest he is resisting a much sharper temptation. Imagine his position—a man of bounding energy, physical, mental, and spiritual, married to a woman old enough to be his mother, and set down in a lonely Cornish parish. Is it strange that he longed for society, for a wider sphere of influence ? " The Tamar Spring " is the record of this crisis in his life, but its meaning is well hidden. A verse of the original MS. omitted in the published version[2] shows he is thinking of preferment in the Church, but we have to apply later words of his own, and some remarks of his friend, Mr. Christopher Harris, to realise the point at issue. It was not that he was overlooked by the Bishop, but that he felt constrained to refuse the offer of a more important living. Mr. Harris tells us that " the late Bishop of Exeter foresaw the bent of his (Hawker's) mind, and offered him a preferment elsewhere, in order, as he told me, to get him away from himself and to hold social communion with others, so as to correct the dogmatism of his own vast and prolific intellect. Hawker in his nature was essentially social, and he dreaded that if he went into the world with his aged wife . . . he might have to resist temptations which it would have been painful to resist, and a dishonour to succumb to. He was in the highest degree attractive to women from his wit, talent and great powers of conversation, besides his extreme good looks."[3] With

[1] " Cornish Ballads," p. 42.
[2] Printed in " Life and Letters," p. 40.
[3] " John Bull," Sept. 25th, 1875.

this to guide us we may read " The Tamar Spring " as
the story of his mental conflict.

Fount of a rushing river ! wild flowers wreathe
　The home where thy first waters sunlight claim ;
The lark sits hushed beside thee while I breathe,
　Sweet Tamar spring ! the music of thy name.

On ! through the goodly channel, on ! to the sea !
　Pass amid heathery vale, tall rock, fair bough :
But never more with footsteps pure and free,
　Or face so meek with happiness as now.

Fair is the future scenery o thy days,
　Thy course domestic, and thy paths of pride :
Depths that give back the soft-eyed violet's gaze,
　Shores where tall navies march to meet the tide.

　　．　　．　　．　　．　　．　　．　　．　　．　　．　　．

Yet false the vision, and untrue the dream,
　That lures thee from thy native wilds to stray :
A thousand griefs will mingle with that stream,
　Unnumbered hearts shall sigh those waves away.

Scenes fierce with men, thy seaward current laves,
　Harsh multitudes will throng thy gentle brink ;
Back ! with the grieving concourse of thy waves,
　Home ! to the waters of thy childhood shrink !

Thou heedest not ! thy dream is of the shore,
　Thy heart is quick with life ; On ! to the sea !
How will the voice of thy far streams implore
　Again amid these peaceful weeds to be !

My Soul ! my Soul ! a happier choice be thine—
　Thine the hushed valley, and the lonely sod ;
False dreams, far vision, hollow hope resign,
　Fast by our Tamar spring, alone with God ! [1]

Far-reaching, indeed, was the effect of this decision
on Hawker's life. He was no ascetic, and no doubt the
fits of morbid despair which clouded his vision were
accentuated by this self-repression. His choice was
ushered in with pain and gloom, for sorrow breathes

[1] " Cornish Ballads," p. 67.

through nearly every poem of this volume. His words on " The Swan," printed in " The South Devon Monthly Museum," May 1st, 1834, seem to be prophetic of his own power of song.

> Heed well the sign !　Oh !　not to Life belong
> The gladdening thoughts that wake my voice of Song !
> When pain can thrill and arrow cleave no more
> Blithe are my hymns along the reedy shore !　[1]

In some of the poems Death itself is the subject, as the priest meets it in his work, as in the heart-broken " Wail of the Cornish Mother " for her lost babe, or the " Death-Song," inspired by the sight—only too frequent—of the corpse of a ship-wrecked sailor washed up on the rocky shore. In others the stress of emotion is not so keen ; an atmosphere of gentle melancholy pervades such poems as " The Ringers of Lancells Tower," or " Trebarrow," where the poet dwells on the thought of passing time, or " Pater Vester Pascit Illa," and " The Sea-Bird's Cry," where he considers the place of the lower animals in the scheme of creation.

As the volume opened, so it closes. The note of resignation is struck again in the last poem, " The Night Cometh."

> What soothes the soul at set of sun ?
> The pleasant thought of duty done.
>
> Yet must the pastoral slumbers be
> The shepherd's by the eastern tree,
> Broken and brief—with dreams that tell
> Of ravaged flock and poisoned well !
>
> Be still, my soul !　fast wears the night
> Soon shall day dawn in holier light.[2]

Whatever minor skirmishes have still to be fought, the main victory has been won. Hawker has chosen a self-denying life of service without recognition, and has put behind him the thought of earthly fame.

[1] " Cornish Ballads," 1908, p. 267.
[2] *Ibid.*, p. 127.

During the next few years he was fully occupied with the work of his parish and various practical undertakings. He spent much thought and energy in building operations, the chief being the new Vicarage. Perhaps he found in this an outlet for artistic expression, for its architecture was certainly singular, and betrayed its builder's originality. Five of the chimneys were " models of Towers of Parish Churches," where he had lived before, and the kitchen chimney represented his Mother's tomb " in its exact shape and dimensions."[1]

He arranged the position of the house, he tells us, so that " the only objects then perceptible from my two fronts will be the Church and the Sea, the suggestions of both which are boundless,"[2] and, no doubt with George Herbert in mind, inscribed over the front door the following verse with its reference to his yearly rent-charge of £365.

> A House, a Glebe, a Pound a Day ;
> A Pleasant Place to Watch and Pray.
> Be true to Church—Be Kind to Poor,
> O Minister ! for evermore.

Self, curbed in one direction, breaks out in another, and Hawker built his house so that it might speak of him—" as, like Absalom, I have no son, I will like him build me a pillar in the Bishop's Dale so that I may be had in Remembrance among men." He had, however, an unselfish motive as well—" I fain would attract too a good man here in every future generation "; and all his other building speaks of his generosity and self-denial. In November, 1837, he writes, " I have finished Combe Bridge, and built an entrance just above my Churchyard Wall, and I am half-way advanced with a Sunday School and Vestiary room, North of the Chancel, to which I have devoted a part of the Materials of my old Vicarage which is taken down."[3] The

---

[1] " Life and Letters," p. 80.
[2] *Ibid.*, p. 77.
[3] *Ibid.*, p. 79.

bridge bears the inscription, " Towards the erection of this bridge built by subscription, in the year of human redemption 1836 his most gracious Majesty, King William the Fourth, gave the sum of Twenty Pounds. Fear God ! Honour the King ! " Mr. Byles, however, quotes the words of the second Mrs. Hawker, written many years later, " The true legend and superscription would be, that, in order to save life—for many men and much cattle had perished in the stream— Robert Stephen Hawker took upon himself the chief cost of the bridge, and let not his left hand know what his right hand had done. And this was a sample of all his doings at Morwenstow."[1] Hawker himself tells us that it was with the help of his " poor dear unselfish and unmurmuring Wife's Portion,"[2] that he was able to do so much.

Hawker's next volume of poems was published in 1840 under the title " Ecclesia," and with the prefatory note, " If I forget thee, O Jerusalem, let my right hand forget her cunning.   If I do not remember thee, let my tongue cleave to the roof of my mouth ; yea, if I prefer not Jerusalem in my mirth." As we should expect from this dedication, many of the seventeen new poems show their author's calling. As a priest he writes on subjects suggested by the Scriptures, or points out the lessons taught by the Catholic Church in building or ritual, but, with the exception of " Morwennae Statio," which he describes as " the only ground wherein this weary heart hath rest," these reveal no secrets of the soul. Two other poems, however, are full of self-revelation. Though they go over ground already trodden in so far as they again describe the poet's mental conflict, they take us further in showing the result of his decision. From " Home Once More " we learn the course of his artistic life.

> Here did I chaunt to many a wind
> The themes of God's eternal mind ;

[1] " Life and Letters," p. 76.
[2] *Ibid.*, p. 82.

While the deep stream and thrilling birds
Made music 'mid those mighty words.

Here oracles an echo found
Breathed, far away on Syrian ground,
By prophet-bards to whom were given
The lore and poetry of Heaven.

Here too would dreamy thoughts recall
Gesture and tone of saintly Paul,
Till fancy heard the iron bands
That shook upon his lifted hands.

All, all is gone—no longer roll
Vision and dream around my soul :
But, in their stead, float down the wind
These fragments of a broken mind.[1]

However much we may regret this self-repression from
the point of view of poetry, it strengthened and deep-
ened his spiritual life, for " The Token Stream of
Tonacombe," though at one point

an image of the days
At duty's loneliest labour meekly bound,

ends with an outburst of mystical fervour at the vision
of the spirit's goal.

Away ! behold at last the torrent leap,
Glad, glad to mingle with yon foamy brine ;
Free and unmourned, the cataract cleaves the steep—
O river of the rocks, thy fate is mine ![2]

This joy after sadness is reflected in two other poems,
for, like Vaughan and Wordsworth, Hawker has begun
to realise the symbolic value of the natural world, and
the song of the cuckoo[3] and the life of the butterfly[4]
foreshadow for him the immortality of the soul.

But before the glad consummation is reached, there
is the long and weary pilgrimage of life. The volume of

[1] " Cornish Ballads," 1908, p. 59.
[2] Ibid., p. 89.
[3] Cf., " I am the Resurrection and the Life ! saith the Lord," " Cornish Ballads," p. 55.
[4] " The Butterfly," " Cornish Ballads," p. 90.

1840 marks a turning-point. Following his inner voice,
Hawker has resigned himself to his round of duties as
a parish priest. He has cut himself off from other minds,
and his vein of ore is almost worked out. Three more
volumes of poems[1] appear before a period of unbroken
silence sets in, but they contain a very small number
of new poems, and show no new inspiration. Though
in the poem on " The Lost Ship : the President," he
re-affirms his steadfast belief in the overshadowing
presence of God, the one new poem with a personal
note is a cry from the depths. The thought of " Words
by the Waters " is " Thou shalt remember the days of
darkness ; for they are many," and the poet, though
the reference in the first edition to I. Kings xix.
shows that the remembrance of that experience " at
the foot of rocky Carradon " is still fresh in his mind,
feels only the weariness of a mortal life which is an
unending struggle between duty and desire.

> Gloom, gloom ! for me—the mountain clothed in cloud,
> The shore of tempests when the storm is loud,
> Where wild winds rush, and broken waters roll,
> And all is dark and stern, like my own wintry soul !
>
> What have I, silvery scene, to do with thee ?
> Mirror of Heaven ! thou glad and glorious sea,
> Thou dost but mock thy wave-worn wanderer's gaze
> With that smooth prophecy of far-off lovelier days.[2]

The preface to " Reeds Shaken with the Wind " of
1843 definitely states, " The Muse of the Priest should
be his Church. It was the beautiful language of the
Sweet Singer of Israel : ' Thy statutes have been my
songs in the house of my pilgrimage,' " and most of
the poems celebrate current events in his parish and
neighbourhood. The years 1841–3 were marked by
several terrible ship-wrecks : the first described by
Hawker, that of " The President," was not on the
Cornish coast, but three other vessels, the " Cale-

---

[1] " Reeds shaken with the Wind," 1843.   Ditto, Second Cluster, 1844.
" Echoes from Old Cornwall," 1846.
[2] " Cornish Ballads," 1908, p. 125.

donia," " Phoenix " and " Alonzo," were cast on the rocks near Morwenstow, and the poem on the figure-head of the " Caledonia " set up at her captain's grave is Hawker's memorial of one. In 1843 he finished the parish school which he had been building, helped by a donation of £15 sent by the Queen Dowager,[1] and wrote a poem for the use of the children, " The Song of the School : St. Mark's, Morwenstow." In the same year he was engaged in a lawsuit to preserve the Well of St. John as Church property, the well and land adjoining having been claimed by Sir J. Y. Buller, and after its successful issue wrote a sonnet on the well and its history.[2] Yet Hawker was too true a poet not to realise how far what he had done fell short of what he might achieve, given the opportunity, and one wonders what was in his mind when he gave a title to these two volumes. Was it that he felt his utterances were but the whispers of " Reeds shaken with the Wind," when they should have been the clarion-call of a prophet ?

He certainly gave himself little time for literary composition, for, besides the work recorded in his poetry, he was instrumental in reviving certain Church activities. He set on foot again customs which had fallen into disuse : Harvest Festivals, and the weekly offertory ; and took part in a somewhat heated correspondence on the latter. As Rural Dean it was through his agency that the first Rural Synod in Eng-land was called together. One extract from the little booklet which he wrote in 1844 on this subject is needed to complete the story of his inner life revealed by his poetry, for it shows the triumph of the devo-tional life :—" I approach this division of my subject with deep and sincere humility of spirit—with an utter prostration of my own thoughts and purposes at the footstool of our Lord and Master Jesus Christ, and with a mere, lowly, single-minded aspiration for the

[1] " Western Luminary," May 9th, 1843.
[2] " Well of St. John," " Cornish Ballads," p. 134.

spiritual welfare of the Church, which is His Body, the pillar and ground of the truth."[1]

After the production of " Echoes of Old Cornwall " in 1846, containing only three new poems, Hawker published no more volumes until 1863. This seems, then, a fitting time to take stock of the impressions already gained. It is clear that we are dealing with a Christian mystic, endowed with a poet's imaginative power and artistic desire for creative self-expression. His outstanding characteristic is energy—of body, mind and spirit. But he develops two sides of his personality at the expense of the third ; his work as Vicar exercises his physical and spiritual powers, while he deliberately holds in check the activities of his imagination. As the result of this is naturally not to be seen in his poetry, we must turn to accounts given by those who knew him to complete the picture of his personality.

[1] " Rural Synods," 1844, p. 10.

CHAPTER II.

PERSONALITY—CHIEFLY AS RECORDED BY FRIENDS.

VERY different is the impression of Hawker gained by studying him in his poetry from that left by his earliest biographer. He is a tragic figure, not a humorous oddity. Yet even Mr. Baring-Gould realised this, though he allowed the fact to be thrust almost out of sight. He describes him as possessing " a character that rolled on its mysterious, unfathomable way," and continues, " To him the spiritual world was intensely real ; he had in him the makings of a mystic ... The spiritual life was the real life : the earthly career was a passing, troubled dream, that teased the soul and broke its contemplations ... The vicar accommodated himself to ordinary society, but he did not belong to it. His spirit hovered high above in the thin, clear air, whilst his body and earthly mind laughed, and joked, and laboured, and sorrowed below. Trouble was the anguish of the soul recalling its prerogative. The fits of depression which came on him were the moments when the soul was asserting its true power, pining as the captive for its home and proper freedom."[1]

Of course, so far as we have seen but one side of Hawker's character. But it has been necessary to begin by emphasizing the serious side of his nature, because he possesses many characteristics which are either so unusual or so unexpected that they thrust themselves to the fore. Immediately, as in Mr. Baring-Gould's book, they assume an importance out of all measure to their worth. Like the odd-shaped pieces of

[1] " Vicar of Morwenstow," ed. 1919, p. 187.

a puzzle, they are without meaning, unless each can be fitted into place to complete the picture. They must be described not for their own sake, but as a further expression of his personality as mystic and artist.

We have seen from the early poetry that the pivot on which Hawker's life revolved was a sense of duty. Based on love, it resulted in whole-hearted service to God and man, and his friends bear witness to its fruits. When he was appointed Vicar of Morwenstow, he came to a parish which had not had a resident Vicar for more than a century. After Hawker's death, a writer in " John Bull " for September 4th, 1875, thus described the result of his labours. " Thirty-three years of patient work, bodily and spiritually, in ceaseless endeavour to do his daily duty . . . changed the bleak wilds of Morwenstow from its savage state into one of the best regulated and most worthily administered parishes in Cornwall." As we have already seen, he had to restore the bridge and build a vicarage and school, and he grudged no expense to set in order and adorn the church. According to the second Mrs. Hawker, " the church was rescued from a state of Puritan desecration, and large sums of money spent upon it, all coming from one source."[1]

His parishioners were " a mixed multitude of smugglers, wreckers and dissenters of various hue,"[2] ignorant and superstitious ; in 1851 they numbered about 1074.[3] Not content with caring only for the welfare of their souls, he followed the example of his grandfather in supplying the needy with food and clothing. One tells us, " No poor man ever came to his door without finding the help which he asked for ; no cottager in the parish but who knew that food and wine were ready for him there, at all times, and in all seasons of distress and sickness,"[4] and another records in 1904 that " some of the old people still living in

[1] " Life and Letters," p. 76.
[2] " Footprints of Former Men." ed, 1908, p. 47.
[3] " Life and Letters," p. 402.
[4] W. Maskell, Pamphlet-reviews from " Athenæum," 1876, p. 18.

Morwenstow have a warm recollection of the Vicar's charity. ' Gude to the poor ! ' cried one old dame, with tears in her eyes. ' His horses might be to the plough, but they must be taken off and sent for Dr. Braund, if he heard there was anybody ill.' "[1] The doctor adds a few words which make it possible for us to imagine the Vicar's sympathy and zeal. " He would be intensely impatient until my arrival, and would walk up and down before the house, saying, ' Why tarry the wheels of Braund's chariot ? ' " Always fettered by lack of money himself, he appreciated its worth to another, and the doctor adds, " He always saw that I was paid." We may see more details in Mr. Baring-Gould's picture. " ' They are crushed down, my poor people,' he would say with energy, stamping about his room —' ground down with poverty, with a wretched wage, the hateful truck system, till they are degraded in mind and body.' It was a common saying of his, ' If I eat and drink, and see my poor hunger and thirst, I am not a minister of Christ, but a lion that lurketh in his den to ravish the poor.' "[2]

Though his attitude was that of the Christian Socialist, he was in no way progressive in politics. He seems to have been strangely out of sympathy with men inspired by the same ideal as himself, F. D. Maurice and Charles Kingsley, for he fears Tennyson cannot be a Religious Man, " being a Maurician,"[3] and Kingsley he calls " Nosey,"[4] evidently a term of rebuke, though it is difficult to see its application. He regarded service as a duty for each individual, and with him charity was not mere alms-giving, but " kindness with God in it."[5] His attitude was like that of Carlyle towards mere philanthropy. To shift the responsibliity from each person to the State was against the teaching of the Gospel, and such views

[1] Byles' "Life and Letters," p. 117.
[2] Baring-Gould, p. 72.
[3] " Life and Letters," p. 415.
[4] Ibid., p. 539.
[5] Ibid., p. 602.

made him oppose innovations in Poor Law adminis-
tration, which we might have expected him to welcome as proofs of a more tender public conscience.
How deeply he felt about them may be gathered from
his remarks in a letter of 1868. " England has never
prospered since the passage of the Poor Law Bill
whereby such direct insult and injury were wrought
upon the Person of the Redeemer of Man. Whatsoever
ye do to the least of these my poor Brethren ye do it
unto me. Lock Him up. Give Him 4 oz. of
Bread."[1] And as poverty in his eyes was sanctified, so
nothing roused him to anger more quickly than mis-
use of this world's goods. Much of the friction between
himself and his parishioners was the result of his plain
speaking on the question of work and wages. He declares in 1864, " There is not a clod in the furrow so
hard as a Farmer's heart."[2] His gentleness and
severity spring from one source.

The sphere of his duties was sometimes extended
to those not of his parish, and his courage at times of
shipwreck is attested in newspaper records. The " Ar-
broath Guide," of September 17th, 1842, speaks of
the burial of ship-wrecked sailors " by direction of
the Rev. Mr. Hawker . . . who has been indefatigable
in his attention on this sad occasion."[3] In the next
year the " Royal Cornwall Gazette " directs " attention to the exertions of the Rev. R. S. Hawker to
extricate the body of a ship-wrecked sailor, whose
head had been forced between the rocks. This good
clergyman thought his time, his anxious superinten-
dence, and his money well bestowed in procuring at
his own expense a number of men and fixing a power-
ful crane, which had to be conveyed from a distance,
to heave the superincumbent mass of rock and extricate the body entire."[4] These bald statements show us

---

[1] " Life and Letters," p. 575.
[2] Ibid., p. 493.   Cf. Hood's indictment earlier (1844) of the farmer in
' Miss Kilmansegg.'
[3] Quoted by Byles, " Life and Letters," p. 161.
[4] Ibid., p. 164.

the energy of the man ; a more detailed picture is
drawn many years later in the " Standard " of September 1st, 1875, by one who writes after Hawker's
death to give his first impressions of Morwenstow and
its Vicar. " The sea was still surly and troubled, with
wild lights breaking over it, and torn clouds driving
through the sky. Up from the shore, along a narrow
path between jagged rocks and steep banks tufted
with thrift, came the Vicar, wearing cassock and sur-
plice, and conducting a sad procession, which bore
along with it the bodies of the two seamen flung up
the same morning on the sands. The office used by
Mr. Hawker at such times had been arranged by himself — not without reference to certain peculiarities
which, as he conceived, were features of the primitive
Cornish Church, the same which had had its bishops
and its traditions long before the conference of Augustine with its leaders under the great oak by the
Severn."[1]

Another of Hawker's characteristics emerges from
this description. His love of the past made him delight
in hunting up forgotten customs, and in keeping alive
dying traditions, which, sometimes, as in the case of
Harvest Festivals and weekly offertories, came to be
generally observed, but more often earned for him a
reputation for singularity. About 1850 he was extreme-
ly interested in " the Greek or Eastern Church, a body
more adverse to Rome than Rome to England,"[2] and
in imitation of the priests of that church he wore a
kind of fez of such a colour that when it had faded
a little he could be described as wearing " a pink hat
without a brim."[3] This he did " to testify the connection of the Cornish Church with the East, before ever
Augustine set foot in Kent."[4]

Though this was the mark of only one phase in his
life, his dress was always somewhat unusual. He has

[1] " Life and Letters," p. 85.
[2] Ibid., p. 86.
[3] Baring-Gould, p. 77.
    Ibid., p. 78

C

recorded his guiding rules in the MS. note, " The two signs are simplicity and value." During the early years of his ministry, his usual out-door clothes were a brown cassock in which he would even scramble up and down the cliffs, a wide-awake beaver hat and Hessian boots. Later, he wore a long purple coat instead of the cassock, and once jokingly told a lady it was " that of an Armenian archimandrite."[1] A fisherman's blue jersey, with a small red cross woven in the side, took the place of a waistcoat, a carpenter's pencil dangled from his button-hole, and he carried a cross-handled walking-stick which he called his pastoral staff. We have learnt enough from his poetry to be able to see the two strands of thought which have produced this result. His artistic nature makes him dislike conventional dress and desire bright colours, while in mystic devotion he seeks to express his ideal of service, by reminding himself that as a follower of Him who was once a Carpenter at Nazareth and who was pierced on the Cross by the " hard centurion's cruel spear," he must be a fisher of men. By 1858 he had found another reason for justifying it. He writes, " You dislike my Garb. Well, I grant a Cassock is not a becoming dress, but the cost is less than £2 a year in lieu of Broadcloth and Coats, and for many years I have paid my Schoolmaster's salary with the difference between the usual price of a Clergyman's coat and my stiff Cassock. The Bills I used to pay when I was a younger fool! And after all when I was full dressed in a Suit of Black Cloth, I was the complete copy of my own Tailor in his gala suit."[2]

But even though we may see the source of his eccentricities we cannot acquit Hawker of a desire to be noticed. It is his old weakness under a new guise. He loved to do things differently from other men, and we may still see the funny side of his singularity. A man who strives to be unconventional must expect to

[1] Baring-Gould, p. 78.
[2] " Life and Letters," p. 85.

be laughed at, for he is often unconsciously humorous.
Incongruity always provokes mirth. Though his own
people accepted his strange clerical costume, he must
have looked a queer figure in the G.W.R. Hotel at
Paddington, and we can understand that friends who
asked to see the clergyman staying there found the
hotel attendants rather obtuse. Indeed, the whole
story of his journey to London for his second marriage
is amusing. He began by stopping the train because he
had lost his brown beaver hat out of the carriage window, and then requested the irate officials to go back
and pick it up. As it was not recovered, at Salisbury
he sent for the stationmaster to ask him where he
could buy hats at the station. He finally arrived in
London with a red handkerchief tied round his head
in place of the lost hat. Even at home he must have
excited smiles, when he rode about his parish in a
poncho, or came down to greet visitors " in a blue
dressing-gown laced with gold braid," and wearing
" red slippers adorned by silver spangles."[1]

But there is no need to exaggerate his singularity.
Some have seen another sign of it in his fondness for
expensive tea, tobacco and stationery. Yet most
people have some pet luxury, and Hawker's were very
natural ones. He paid 5/4 a lb. for his tea from Twining's, smoked pure Latakia in short, large-bowled clay
pipes, and had his note paper made specially for him
by Messrs. De la Rue. But he considered he had a
right to indulge in these luxuries, for, " as I have not
tasted Fermented Fluids for a great number of years,"
he writes, " my Stationery is my Wine."[2] His pens,
paper and ink formed one of the means by which he
expressed himself, and were therefore of great importance. He saw his writing as representative of
himself. Just as the frequent capitals are part of his
style, so the paper " thick and parchment-like, and
ruled with faint red lines," the Swanquills, and

[1] " Life and Letters," p. 607, note.
[2] *Ibid.*, p. 88.

" Black Ink of the old kind " are part of his individuality. He had pleasure in his " own Autograph," and delight in his cipher R.S.H.,[1] while an added distinction was given by his seals. In these his love of symbolism re-appears, for his favourite ones were the Pentacle of Solomon and the mystic Fish.

A man whose ordinary dress was so full of symbolic meaning would naturally delight in ecclesiastical vestures. What his enemies called Romanising practices were in Hawker simply the outcome of his desire for beauty in outward show and hidden meaning, and of his love of the past. But they naturally excited some remark, for he was one of the first Anglican clergy to revive the use of elaborate vestments. They were not, as for the Tractarians, the accessories to a plan of campaign, but the expression of his personality. A picture of Hawker as priest is drawn by the Rev. W. Haslam in his book, " From Death unto Life." " On the Sunday," he says, " I was asked to help him in the service, and for this purpose was arrayed in an alb, plain, which was just like a cassock of white linen. As I walked about in this garb, I asked a friend, ' How do you like it ? ' In an instant I was pounced upon and grasped sternly on the arm by the Vicar. ' Like has nothing to do with it ; is it right ? ' He himself wore over his alb a chasuble, which was amber on one side and green on the other, and was turned to suit the Church seasons ; also a pair of crimson-coloured gloves, which he contended were the proper sacrificial colour for a priest."[2] Mrs. Waddon Martyn of Tonacombe Manor describes how Mr. Hawker christened her eldest son " in full vestments as he always did— alb, magnificent purple velvet cope, fastened with a large sort of brooch—a white stole very richly worked in gold, an exact copy, he said, of St. Cuthbert's found on opening the coffin still preserved (in Durham Cath-

---

[1] *V.* J. T. Blight's " Ancient Crosses and other Antiquities in the South and East of Cornwall," and " Week at the Land's End." Hawker's contributions are all signed with his monogram.

[2] Haslam, " From Death unto Life," p. 38.

edral)."[1] The motive behind this is revealed by a MS. note dated 1838. " What were the Ornaments of Ministers in the 2nd year of King Edward VI ? Find and use," followed by the words, "(Added.) I have done this eleven years. 1849. R.S.H."[2]

His use of symbolism—at first, for him, as for all mystics, a medium of expression, was too soon degraded. It became almost a fetish, and his idiosyncrasy affected even the services which he conducted. Strangers must have found his procedure somewhat alarming, for the following is an account of an ordinary Sunday Service. " The Vicar inside the dim chancel was concealed from the congregation by the screen. He would wander up and down the chancel, book in hand, and reading now in English, now in Latin. At certain points in the service he would prostrate himself on the ground before the Altar, with outstretched arms, in the form of a cross. A little door in the screen gave access to the pulpit, and the Vicar had great difficulty in squeezing through. When asked why he did not enlarge the door, he would say, ' Don't you see that this typifies the camel going through the eye of the needle ? ' After the sermon he came down the pulpit steps backward, finding that the only possible way of returning through the door. Strangers preaching at Morwenstow who did not know of this device, would find themselves imprisoned on the stairs, till the Vicar came to their rescue. ' It is the strait and narrow way,' he would whisper, ' and few there be that find it.' "[3] Towards the end of his life, the pulpit was lowered by his assistant, Mr. Rawlins, and the Vicar was much troubled. " I always regarded the sermon," he said, " as tidings from on high."[4]

These original additions to a form of service already rich in symbolic meaning were not the only signs of Hawker's unusual views. His intense realisation of the

[1] " Life and Letters," p. 134.
[2] Ibid., p. 127.
[3] Ibid., p. 144.
[4] Ibid., p. 604.

presence of God everywhere, a sense as vivid and abiding for him as it was for Blake, led him to make less distinction between being in church or out of church than is the general custom. The church itself was only a symbol, and all the world was holy ground. He loved the building for its message from the past, but it asked of him no more reverence than " every tree, animal and rock." He was the man as well as the priest, and saw nothing incongruous in his gift of a piece of barley-sugar to the churchwarden's little niece when she handed the list of hymns to him through the screen,[1] and nothing unfitting in somewhat pointed references in sermons to members of the congregation.

The writer in the " Standard " describes another custom. " In Mr. Hawker's judgment all the creatures had a certain right of admission to God's house. He sometimes appeared at his lectern attended by four or five cats, unusual but graceful acolytes, who, as he assured us, allowing for an occasional display of youthful vivacity, rarely conducted themselves otherwise than with great propriety. A clergyman to whom he showed the church writes, " I wanted to shut out my dog, but he insisted on his coming in, as much more fit than many Christians."[2] His whole attitude towards animals was that of the mystic who, convinced of the unity underlying all creation, looked on the lower orders of life with an enlightened vision, and was ever seeking to find a message for mankind symbolised in animal or bird or flower. He had in small measure the quality which was so marked in St. Francis of Assisi. We are told that " he had a wonderful power over animals. When driving, he kept the reins loose, and talked all the time to his horses, who seemed to understand him and did whatever he told them,"[3] and we learn, too, that " the wild birds would

[1] " Life and Letters," p. 145.
[2] *Ibid.*, p. 108.
[3] *Ibid.*, p. 108.

flutter round him as he stood calling them all by name,
' Jacky, Tommy, Robin,' and feeding them with
crumbs from his hand."¹ Hawker himself adds a delightful touch in his description of a " Scarecrow put
up by my old Man," which " was so made up in my
hat and broken Cassock that they took it for me, and
came around it looking up to be fed."² Birds and
animals were his friends, for " here within the ark,"
he writes in 1850, " we hear only the voices of animals
and birds and the sound of many waters."³ Early in
his career, he had some rather unusual pets, one of
which was a " black pig of Berkshire breed, well cared
for, washed and currycombed, which ran beside him
when he went out for walks and paid visits. It was
called Gyp, and was intelligent and obedient."⁴ A
second Herrick and his pig ! Not so well-trained, however, were the two stags, Robin Hood and Maid
Marian, which he kept in the combe in front of the
house ; Mr. Baring-Gould tells two stories of their
fierce behaviour to visitors, and even the vicar himself seems to have had to use force towards them.⁵

One could add many examples of his feeling for
animals and birds, for his letters are full of references
to his farm, and one written in 1866 shows very clearly
the place it occupied in his thought. The letter opens
with some remarks on speakers in a Parliamentary
debate, Lytton Bulwer, Lowe, Stanley and Mill, but
continues with details of events on the farm, and
though the writer is jesting at the end of his account,
he is quite serious when he leaves one subject for the
other with the words, " I turn from these trivial
topics to those of graver import, our animals and
Birds."⁶ The beasts gave him the affection which he
craved, on earth, and the birds reminded him of

---

¹ " Life and Letters," p. 103.
² *Ibid.*, p. 104.
³ Baring-Gould, p. 147.
⁴ *Ibid.*, p. 22.
⁵ *Ibid.*, p. 57.
⁶ " Life and Letters," p. 542.

spiritual companionship, for, as he delighted to repeat, " Ubi aves ibi Angeli." It was, indeed, as he
himself says, his " almost slang saying,"[1] and as he
grew older, it was but a step for him to believe in
birds of good and evil omen. Superstition flourishes
among men who live close to nature, and the Cornish
country-side is one of its strong-holds.

We cannot deny that Hawker's beliefs gradually
became stranger and more extravagant. Gifted as he
was with vivid imagination, and at the same time,
deficient in a sense of humour, it was the most natural
development, for he himself had turned his imagination back from its true outlet in poetry. He could not
restrain its activity, however, and it led him into
strange places. He was peculiarly sensitive, as we
have seen in his poetry, to spiritual influences, and
his imagination, having nothing better to do, delighted in presenting these in bodily form. He writes,
in all seriousness, of an encounter with a Brownie, " a
swift, brown, rough shape," which " started up
among the gorse bushes, and rushed or glided towards the stream,"[2] and as early as 1838 explains how
a ghost may appear, for " Sir Walter Scott's White
Lady of Avenel is an exact delineation of the Scholas-
tic Spirit of Hades or purgatorial fiend. A Kind of
Elastic Vapour compressed in order to be tangible to
the eye and then dilated to vanish into thin air."[3]
There is no insistence on Hawker's part that these
things are seen with " the eye of the mind," as the
mystics are so careful to do with true visions, and as
Hawker himself does, in his real spiritual experiences,
and we cannot but regret these shadows which shut
out the light. Instead of thought purified in the re-
fining fire of poetry, we have it mingled with the alloy
of superstition. Mr. Byles declares that the Vicar
" shared to no small extent . . . the native belief in

[1] " Life and Letters," p. 518.
[2] *Ibid.*, p. 100.
[3] " Stones Broken from the Rocks," p. 37.

such things as witchcraft, omens, the evil-eye, ill-wishing, ghosts, fairies, pixies and mermaids," but that it was often difficult for his hearers to decide whether he was serious in his statements. He once said to a friend, who called, " Did you meet a wag-gonette full of people ? I stuffed them up with all kinds of nonsense, and they believed every word ! "[1]

In spite of this Hawker's own actions and words prove that he readily absorbed the traditions and beliefs of his parishioners, and held to them as staunchly as the most ignorant peasant. Like Herrick, he was interested in their charms and spells, for not only did he make notes of charms to cure the thrush, for sleepy foot, for cramp, and to make butter come, but even used them himself. An organist and music-master, who, on his professional journeys often stayed at Morwenstow, gave the following account of his first visit. " I had retired to rest, then just after one o'clock in the morning. The Rev. gentleman entered my bed-room, and solemnly addressing me, said, now was the hour to confess my sins which (as he said) were many. If I would repeat the following words three times and have faith, it would prove an infallible remedy to exorcise all evil spirits :—

> Clean birds by sevens,
> Unclean by twos.
> The Dove in the Heavens
> Is the one I will choose."[2]

His belief in witchcraft, the evil eye and ghosts was not simulated. The grounds of his belief are set down in his notes, and in addition we learn that " whenever he met anyone who, as he thought, had an evil eye, he would move the fingers of his left hand into a certain position supposed to act as a counter-charm. The first and fourth fingers were held straight and stiff, the second and third bent inwards on the palm, with the

[1] " Life and Letters," p. 99.
[2] *Ibid.* p. 102.

thumb folded across them."[1] At his meeting with the
Brownie he remembered " that every spirit must
crouch to the Sign," and so " made it in the air,"[2]
while Mr. Baring-Gould records that with one of his
seals, the pentacle of Solomon, he claimed that he
could command the devils.[3] Such is the degraded work
in store for the imagination of a poet if it fails to per-
form its allotted task.

But in spite of its vagaries, Hawker's imagination
was responsible for much of the charm which he exer-
cised on all who came into contact with him. All his
friends testify to the delight which they felt in his
company. The writer in the " Standard " declares
that " it was a pleasure of no common kind to wander
with him through the woods of Stowe or along the
high downs overlooking the sea. Story after story,
verse after verse, came pouring forth at every moment." How much we have lost because there was no
Boswell among Hawker's friends to preserve his conversation ! We should have seen his rare gift of
sympathy at its best, as he talked with his equals,
encouraged the poor, told stories to the children ; we
should have delighted in his ready wit, and his keen
sense of the dramatic ; above all, we should have detected the wistful note underlying all his fun, and
have realised that the pain gnawing at his heart was
that endured by the man who cannot understand himself. For Hawker can be called a humorist only in the
old sense of being a " fantastical or whimsical person.'
He was deft at repartee, for he had an alert brain and
a quick perception of the ridiculous, but he lacked one
thing. Though he had also imagination and sympathy,
he was not gifted with that elusive quality which re-
solves them all into a sense of humour. There is a
wall of partition between his laughter and his tears ;
though he passes rapidly from one to the other, they

---

[1] " Life and Letters," p. 66.
[2] *Ibid.*, p. 100.
[3] " Vicar of Morwenstow," p. 79.

never merge ; his humour is never the twin of pathos, nor his sorrow lightened by a smile at his own weakness. Hawker is often unconsciously humorous because he never laughed at himself. He took himself far too seriously, and seems to have bewitched all his friends into taking his jesting for granted. For instance, the following description of him is given by Mr. Maskell. " No man was more apt . . . in impressing strangers with an idea of his extensive knowledge ; and he would occasionally not only draw upon what stock he did possess but would give some famous name as an authority for what had sprung solely from his own clever brain. He seldom ventured upon this when there was a chance of being found out, but if detected would enjoy the experiment."[1]

But in this there can be no doubt that imagination was the servant of memory, for Hawker's brain was " a snapper-up of unconsidered trifles," and delighted in making use of stores it already possessed. He was fully aware of its tendency himself, and had a horror of unconscious plagiarism, so that in his published writings he was on the alert to avoid repetition of thought or phrase, and careful to note quotation. But his letters had no such safe-guard, and show that it was his memory rather than his invention which was at work. We find that his favourite statement, "Ubi Aves ibi Angeli," was a phrase wherein he " had condensed a theory of Ephrem Syrus years ago, but which Eph. Sy. never wrote."[2] We find him writing a letter to accompany the gift of a honey-comb to Sir T. Acland, and solemnly stating that " when our bees, on forage, are caught there by a sudden storm, they stoop down, gather up a small pebble or stone for ballast in the wind, and so glide safely home to their hive, where they drop it at the door. This is one of the bits of natural History which one gathers from an out-of-door life by the Sea."[3] Can we doubt that Hawker had

[1] Maskell, p. 7.
[2] " Life and Letters," p. 519.
[3] *Ibid.*, p. 244.

travelled over the same ground as Richard Rolle of
Hampole, who basing his statements on Pliny's
" Natural History " had written in the fourteenth
century of the bee, " when scho flyes, scho takes erthe
in hyr fete that scho be noghte lyghtly overheghede in
the ayere of wynde."[1] So must it have been with much
that his hearers thought quaint and original, and we
can quite understand that the " habit of hoaxing became so ingrained in his nature that perhaps, as he
grew older, he was hardly able himself to distinguish
between jest and earnest, fact and fancy, belief and
simulated belief."[2]

But if Hawker lacked real humour, he had the
quick and agile mind which wit demands. He was an
adept at seizing the moment for a witty repartee or a
remark charged with hidden meaning, as on the occasion when he whispered to his old college friend,
Jeune, who as Dean of Magdalen Hall was leading a
rather plump gentleman-commoner to present him to
the Vice-Chancellor, " Why, your peg's surely mazed,
maister." This cryptic remark completely upset the
Dean's gravity by reminding him of incidents which
occurred after they as undergraduates had set free all
the pigs of Boscastle.[3] Another instance of a ready
answer is the one given to an inquisitive tourist who
wished to know his views and opinions. Taking him to
a window in the passage facing the sea, Hawker remarked, " There is Hennacliff, the highest cliff on this
coast, on the right ; the church on the left ; the Atlantic Ocean in the middle. These are my views. My
opinions I keep to myself."[4] His power of making a
word a double-edged weapon naturally resulted in a
love of epigram, and some verses of this type have been
printed among his poems. One of the wittiest, however, occurs only in the " Life and Letters." Hearing
an election candidate declare with great emphasis, " I

[1] E.E.T.S., Eng. Prose Treatises of R. Rolle of Hampole, p. 8.
[2] " Life and Letters," p. 99.
[3] V. Hawker's own description in " Footprints," p. 191 ff.
[4] " Life and Letters," p. 92.

will never be priest-ridden ! " Hawker hastily wrote
and handed to him the words,

> Thou ridden ! no ! that shall not be,
> By prophet or by priest !
> Balaam is dead, and none but he
> Could choose *thee* for his beast ! [1]

The whimsical side of his character was shown in
his actions as well as his speech. Professor Saintsbury
states that Hawker " was old enough to belong to the
days of literary mystification,"[2] but we need not hunt
for a link with Chatterton or Macpherson. His little
habit of publishing poems anonymously and then pro-
ceeding to use much paper and ink in proving his
authorship can be traced to two strands in his character. It pandered to his sense of fun, and it gratified his
vanity, for to be in possession of information which no
one else had, and to have attention focussed on oneself when others did in time gain the knowledge, gave
one a very pleasant feeling of superiority. It had the
disadvantage, however, of making the author subordinate to his poem, and the note of wounded vanity
is sounded in Hawker's remarks on the " Trelawny
Ballad." This is the best-known of his poems partly
because the discussion as to how much of it Hawker
did write recurred at intervals for many years, but
the history of the " Christ-Cross Rhyme " is an even
better example of his painstaking endeavours to cover
his tracks, and afterwards to prove his identity. The
poem was first published in 1846 with an illustration
in a little volume entitled " Poems and Pictures."
In 1854 he writes to " Notes and Queries," " Suffer me
to reply to a question . . . about a ' Christ-cross row.'
This name for the alphabet obtained in the good old
Cornish dame schools when I was a boy. In a book
that I have seen there is a vignette of a monk teaching
a little boy to read, and beneath, ' A Christ-Cross
Rhyme.' " He concludes by quoting his own lines.

[1] " Life and Letters," p. 94.
[2] Camb. Hist. of Eng. Lit., vol. XII., p. 134.

Two years passed before this bore any fruit, but in 1856 a correspondent to " Willis's Current Notes " sent a version of the poem, with the remark, " These met my eye the very day in which I saw those of the Rev. R. S. Hawker in C.N. I strongly suspect the two canticles are derived from a common source." Hawker then was able to write an indignant letter to claim the poem. With what relish he must have set down the words, " It is time to put a stop if possible to the daring robbery perpetrated on my Brain and pen and that continually."[1] It was a harmless outlet for his pugnacious instincts.

These were not always so easily satisfied. Hawker had the hot temper and the dogged tenacity of the fighter. Possessing a strong will and decided views of his own, he is seen at his worst at times when he has to face opposition. He was too forceful in every way to be diplomatic in his relations with his opponents, and Mr. Byles even goes as far as to say " he was a good hater, open and above-board in his enmity, not nourishing a secret grudge, nor speaking behind a man's back what he would not say to his face. It was this quality which won the respect of those whom he most denounced, and moved them to speak well of him after his death."[2] Yet it is surely safe to say that he never hated any person. He found himself so often in opposition to the views of those around him, and his deep-set belief in himself as the servant of God made him denounce them as enemies of the truth. He quarrelled violently with the farmers in his parish, but it was because he found them selfish and avaricious; he spared no words to express his hatred of Wesleyanism for the emphasis it laid on mere emotion, and the degraded thought which had crept into its teaching, but yet we are told that "his relations with Dissenters in his parish were very friendly, though he was so bluntly outspoken for the church."[3] At one time one

[1] " Life and Letters," pp. 259, 260.
[2] Ibid., p. 150.
[3] Ibid., p. 154.

of his churchwardens was " a Wesleyan and local preacher," who was also " one of the largest Farmers in Morwenstow."[1] He was not so intolerant as his words appear, though sometimes he does seem to exult over the downfall of his enemies in the most unchristian manner. In 1850, for instance, he writes, " Fifteen years I have been vicar of this altar, and all that while no lay person, landlord, tenant, parishioner or steward, has ever proffered me even one kind word, much less aid or corn. Nay, I have found them all bristling with dislike. All the great men have been hostile to me in word or deed. Yet I thank my Master and His angels, I have accomplished in and around my church a thousand times more than the great befriended clergy of this deanery. Not one thing has failed. When I lack aid to fulfil, I go to the altar and ask it. Is it conceded ? So fearfully that I shudder with thanksgiving. A person threatened me with injury on a fixed day. I besought rescue. On that very day that person died. A false and treacherous clergyman came to a parish close by. I shook with dread. I asked help. It came. He entered my house five days afterwards to announce some malady unaccountable to him. He went. It grew. He resigned his cure last week. And these are two only out of forty miracles."[2] This shows Hawker at his worst, a being compounded of spiritual pride and diseased imagination, and without the slightest touch of humour.

But after all, these were only phases in his life, the utterances of times when he was in the grip of black melancholy, and, though we need never doubt Hawker's sanity, there was much in his outlook which came near the morbidity of an unhinged mind. He knew it himself, for in 1864 he writes, " God keep me safe in my mental powers. I have a terrible dread of losing power over my own mind. Like Dean Swift I have a horror of becoming ' a spectacle to men.' "[3] The latter

[1] " Life and Letters," p. 155.
[2] Baring-Gould, p. 143.
[3] " Life and Letters," p. 487.

part of his life was too often clouded, as we shall see, by fits of intense depression, and the twist of nature which allowed him at these times to rejoice over the defeat of his enemies is put in its best light by his friend, Mr. Maskell. "Robert Hawker's imagination often ran away with him, and he would, undoubtedly, connect such occurrences in his own mind and speak of them as if they were the consequences in the way of miracle, of injuries done to himself. But he was the last man in the world to have wished evil to another ; his whole life was an example of constant kindness to everyone and of excess of hospitality wherever and whenever it was in his power ; and his bitterest enemy would have been certain to receive shelter and help and food."[1]

Every man has his failings, but only in the strongest characters is the contrast between weak and strong points so marked, and the conflict between them so intense. It is difficult to draw the character of Hawker with due regard to proportion. Yet surely with the remembrance of the early poetry in our minds, we may see the real man. He was one who, in his own words, tried to " cherish a Spirit of Sacrifice, i.e., a Bent Mind," to "wish what God wishes."[2] All the anomalies in his character are explained by this, and his eccentricities fall into place. They are like the berries of the misletoe plant, which springs from an apple-tree, insignificant compared with its true fruit, yet calling attention to themselves from their rare growth. Yet they derive their life from the same source, and as all Hawker's work of value to the world springs from the fact that he was at once a mystic and an artist, so does this same fact lie at the root of many of his eccentricities. For Hawker failed to bring the two sides of his character into harmony with each other. In Blake, great mystic and great artist, the fusion of the two was so perfect that his life was one of deep joy and

[1] Maskell, p. 16.
[2] " Life and Letters, p. 129.

serene peace ; Hawker was torn in two by the conflict. Finally, the mystic in him triumphed at the expense of the artist, and his creative energy, balked in
one direction, sought new outlets. Untutored by a
sense of humour, it made him an eccentric.

His own words, written of the Cornish clergy before
his time, may well end this chapter, for he too " became developed about middle life into an original
mind and man, sole and absolute within his parish
boundary, eccentric when compared with his brethren
in civilised regions, and yet, in German phrase, ' a
whole and seldom man ' in his dominion of souls."[1]

[1] "Footprints," p. 159.

D

CHAPTER III.

1846-75. LIFE AND CHARACTER (*continued*).

WE must take up the story of Hawker's life after the publication of his last volume of collected poems, " Echoes of Old Cornwall," in 1846. Our path is no longer that of the explorer. From the poetry of his youth and early manhood we have been able to trace the development of Hawker's mind and character, and the picturesque details supplied by those who knew him have completed the portrait. Now his character is set, his ideals are formed, and his environment is such that he has no new sources of inspiration. In the solitude of his Cornish village, his mind is turned in on itself, and, as far as literary production is concerned, many years pass in silence unbroken save by a few fragments of prose and verse, stamped sometimes too deeply with the impress of their author's strong personality. But though he printed little, he wrote much, and a number of MS. notebooks,[1] and nearly a thousand letters, remain to throw light on the phases of his literary activity. For this second period there is much more material to work upon, but it is impossible to make the story of Hawker's later life as interesting as that of his early days. It is a record of great powers wasted, of opportunities lost—in short, as he himself says, of " a most unavailing life."[2] The chief elements in it were sadness and monotony. We feel that a shadow has fallen across the man, and only occasionally do

---

[1] Now in the possession of Mr. Byles, through whose courtesy I have been able to consult them.
[2] " Life and Letters," p. 401.

the clouds part to let the sunlight through. The words in which Coleridge described his dejection are true of Hawker's later life.

> But now afflictions bow me down to earth :
> Nor care I that they rob me of my mirth ;
> But oh ! each visitation
> Suspends what nature gave me at my birth,
> My shaping spirit of Imagination.

Hawker sought relief in the same way as Coleridge did, though his use of opium does not seem to have affected his writings. We find no record of visions of " the cloud-capped towers, the gorgeous palaces," such as Coleridge and De Quincey saw while under its influence.

The two sources of information for this period of Hawker's life are complementary to each other. The note-books show the workings of his mind, the letters for the most part record his experiences, though some, of course, give the result of his meditation. In the one we see the energy of an active imagination dissipated, and therefore almost entirely unfruitful; in the letters we see the causes and the results of this, as he discusses practical details with his brother and his friends, or reveals the secrets of his spiritual experience to persons whom he had never met in the flesh. The notes which were at first chiefly on religious subjects, become more discursive about 1846, but more of his life is shown by the letters, which fortunately have been preserved from that date. Almost all the earlier ones are lost.

After the publication of " Echoes of Old Cornwall," we have to account for a period of silence, for nothing more is printed till 1849. It is not difficult to find the reason, for Hawker was passing through a time of great anxiety. In 1856 he describes this crisis in his life. " One clear, plain and mournful Statement will record a volume—Not only was every morsel of their[1]

---

[1] The Misses I'ans—his wife's sisters.

land sold for the behoof of claimants, but Mrs. Hawker and myself had to surrender her annuity from leaseholds to meet so far as its estimated value would go the surplusage of debt, and I myself incurred and have gradually paid several hundred pounds. This climax occurred about ten years agone. At that advanced period of my own life, a still more advanced one of several years in my Wife's case, we had as it were to begin that tragedy called Life over again."[1] Letters written during the time of strain show his state of mind : " I have been literally hunted by hounds from Stratton and the neighbourhood so as to poison all my peace."[2] " I have gone through a very bitter time of it... Think what I must have suffered."[3] " I have been bitterly dealt with."[4]

Yet his imagination must have been still active in spite of these difficulties, for whatever the truth of the matter may be, Hawker undoubtedly composed about 116 lines on the adventures of Prince Charlie after the battle of Culloden. This subject was set for the Newdigate Prize Poem in 1847, and the successful competitor was a pupil of Hawker's. We shall never know whether Hawker had previously conceived a poem on this subject and was already at work on it, or, hearing the subject and being attracted by it, amused himself by turning out lines on Prince Charlie, but it is clear from both internal and external evidence that the poem as it stands is as much his as its reputed author's. We cannot think that this was done with Hawker's connivance, and may perhaps see in the resentment which he felt at lines of his composition winning " praise in another's name,"[5] another reason for the complete cessation from literary work which marks

1 " Life and Letters," p. 282.
2 Unpublished letter undated—probably 1845.
3 April, 1846.
4 January, 1847.
5 Brit. Mus. MS. 37, 825, contains a copy of the Prize Poem : " Prince Charles after Culloden," in which Hawker has marked some lines, and a letter in which he speaks of them as " lines of my own which once won praise in another's name."

these years. Words written in 1850 may refer to this pupil and his brother,[1] who, Hawker felt, had treated him with " gross ingratitude " in other matters in which he had worked on their behalf. He writes, " When I look around I see many like Frankenstein whom I have moulded from clay into life, and who turn and rend me."[2]

The natural effect of anxieties piled one above another was physical and mental exhaustion. In 1848 Hawker had a serious illness, followed by a time of intense depression. In February he writes in the depth of morbid despair, " Never yet was a man crushed as I have been . . . I have not smiled for months . . . I loathe life, and I yearn for death as some men do for wealth or rank."[3] This cry becomes more poignant as the years pass. We hear it again in one of the poems written in the next year.

> Here by the lonely Severn sea,
> I, too, have borne, years fierce and long,
> All hatred and rebuke and wrong.[4]

And the poem in which these words occur is a most significant one. It was written to encourage the Protestant Sisters of Mercy at Devonport, who had been accused, falsely, as was later proved, of Romanising practices. We see Hawker setting out on the road of theological discussion, always a thorny one, but especially so to many of the Victorians. Moreover it shows that he had chosen a dim-eyed leader, for a note refers to " the works of Gretser published in Latin, in seventeen folio volumes at Ratisbon 1734—41."[5] The other poems of this year show that he is

[1] Of the latter Hawker writes that he " had induced Dinham to give him his nominal articles so that he might go up for examination as a Medical Man." Letter 21.
[2] " Life and Letters," p. 203.
[3] *Ibid.*, p. 188.
[4] " Cornish Ballads," p. 140.
[5] Jacob Gretser (1561—1625), German theologian of the order of Jesuits, was for 24 years professor at Ingolstadt, where he lectured on philosophy, morality and school-divinity. He also published more than 150 works, most of them in defence of the Jesuits and against Protestant authors.

more concerned with details of Church government
than with the realities of life. Though in an undated
poem which probably belongs to this time, for it refers
to an occasion " when Rogues in Sermons sue that
captive Maids may fall,"[1] he seems to deplore the
waste of time spent in argument, the poem on " St.
Andrew's Day " is only an appeal for examination of
methods.

> What is our vision ? what the crafty toil
> Whereby to win the draught and share the spoil ?

he asks, and finds the answer in the Gospel story.

> Simon and Andrew sate, and calm on board
> *Mended their nets*—and waited for the Lord ! [2]

Surely a subject bristling with points for debate !

During the next few years we see Hawker's imagination losing touch more rapidly with real life. Anxieties
—with reference to money, health, theology—fasten
him to earth, and his imagination, lacking creative
energy, roams ineffectively over the most diverse subjects in heaven and earth. The linking of matter and
spirit is a mystery on which his mind delights to
linger, and he writes note after note of philosophical
speculation, dogmatic theology or fantastic symbolism which bear on this.[3] The Incarnation is the pivot
round which his thought revolves, and the idea of the
Virgin Mary becomes almost an obsession. He finds
relief from the trials of the present in images of the
past or the future, and appears in print only as an
antiquarian searching for literary fossils in the shape
of story or custom. In 1850 he began to contribute to
" Notes and Queries " : he sent two paragraphs on
burial customs,[4] one on the popular dislike to burial
on the north side of the church, the other on burial
towards the west, a query on " Combs buried with

---

[1] *V.* Two verses of the 2nd version of " Sir Hugh," " Cornish Ballads."
p. 287.
[2] " Cornish Ballads." p, 142.
[3] Unpublished MS. notebooks.
[4] " Notes and Queries," II., pp. 253, 408.

the Dead,"[1] and a little Morality, " The First Mole in
Cornwall."[2] But that is all there is to show for the
year, though the desire to write was strong. " Were it
not for the bad base worry of my post-bag," he cried
to his brother, " I could write a Volume of MS. every
night."[3]

No doubt a statement written in 1854 accounts for
some of the worry. " Many years ago, or rather in
1850, said Pattison to me—' You must pay this money
or —— swears he will pursue you until he has seques-
trated your living and utterly ruined you. You cannot
assuage his revenge but by payment.' I agreed and
paid him."[4] But he could increase his salary only by
doing more work, and he therefore took the curacy of
Welcombe, three miles from Morwenstow, in addition
to his own charge, and held a service there every Sunday between the two services at Morwenstow. It was
a crucial time, too, in the Church of England. Since
the secession to Rome in 1844 and 1845 of some of the
chief figures in the Oxford Movement, there had been
much searching of heart among members of the Anglican communion, and one event in particular must
have closely affected Hawker. His friend, William
Maskell, examining chaplain to the Bishop of Exeter,
joined the Church of Rome in 1850 after the Gorham
judgment, a case in which the Bishop's decision was
annulled by the action of a civil court, and, though
Hawker touches lightly on the question,[5] it must have
troubled him to a certain extent. There were also the
claims of Rome to be considered, for in 1850 Pope
Pius IX. created a new Roman Catholic hierarchy in
England. It is small wonder that Hawker failed to pro-

[1] " Notes and Queries," p. 230.
[2] Ibid., p. 225.
[3] " Life and Letters," p. 202.
[4] Ibid., p. 234.
[5] " The Church horizon seems dark. But I do not think there was
any warranty for secession in the Gorham Events. The decision of the
Privy Council did not alter the position of a single Priest. Their departure
seems to me more like pique because they could not have their own way
than anything else." " Life and Letters," p. 204.

duce imaginative work during these years. Some time during 1851 he must have fallen ill under the strain, for he writes in 1860, " When I was so ill, and so near death in 1851 Dr. Budd told Mrs. Hawker that he had never encountered in all his practice so excitable a tissue as that which held my Brain. He hinted that any great trial or sorrow would in all likelihood overwhelm my mind . . . I refer to this peculiar texture my wakefulness at night. A cross parishioner or an angry correspondent has power over my sleep a whole night.[1]

All that appeared in print were answers to two questions in " Notes and Queries " on " the ring-finger" and "dole-bank,"[2] though he writes to his brother in November, " What a thought it is to think that about £600 would unshackle my mind, nerve my heart, enable me to work with MSS. such as no other Man in England has . . . But regret is mere and fruitless."[3] He is indeed in the slough of despond, and though he writes in the notes, " Of all lives the saddest is a purposeless aimless existence,"[4] we feel that he is allowing himself to be beaten down by " the slings and arrows of outrageous fortune." A letter written some years later must refer to this time. " Anxiety, domestic and other kinds, and Griefs many subdued me, and my chief thought came, Where most peacefully could I die ? Where be most tranquilly buried ? and so I gathered inwards every thought, every hope, and became as I am now rooted to my own graveside without an external plan or desire."[5] We feel exasperated that a man of only 48 should be willing to give up the struggle so tamely.

Fortunately the next year his affairs took a turn for the better. He made several new friendships, though only through the medium of letters. So vivid was Hawker's perception of spirit, that he seems to have

---

[1] " Life and Letters," p. 328.
[2] " Notes and Queries," IV., pp. 199, 213.
[3] " Life and Letters," p. 217.
[4] Unpublished.
[5] " Life and Letters," p. 360.

been able to recognise a kindred soul from afar, and to have been willing to reveal himself to one whom he had never met in the flesh. Certainly the letters written in 1852 to the Rev. William West and the Twinings are among the most intimate he ever wrote, and he knew Mr. West only as the contributor " Eirronach " in " Notes and Queries," and Mr. Twining as the head of the firm from which he bought his tea wholesale, though Miss Twining had written two books—" Symbols and Emblems of Early and Mediæval Christian Art," and " Types and Figures of the Bible "—on subjects in which Hawker was interested. We must turn to letters to these friends to see the course of Hawker's spiritual life. In September 1852 he writes to Miss Twining, " You refer to the MS. extracts which I transcribed for you some time ago. Their history is this : I have kept on my table for many years a Thought-Book in which I write down every reference, question and idea worth preserving which may come to me in course of reading or meditation. The latter which I practise in my Chancel—alone and often at night—is my most abundant source of instruction. There mysteries are made clear, doctrines illustrated, and tidings brought, which I firmly believe are the work of angelic ministry. Of course the angels of the altar are there and the angel of my own baptism is never away."[1]

Even more illuminating is the long letter written in December 1852 to the Rev. William West. After describing an occasion on which he read the " Exorcistic service of the Western Church in Latin " over a rebellious Vestry with the result that the evil spirits inhabiting five farmers " fled from the room howling," Hawker gives an account of two mystic experiences. He writes of the second of these, " I remember once I was earnest to be told in what manner and way The Great Change was wrought in Chancels when the Mighty One descends. Deep in Thought I saw, not

[1] " Life and Letters," p. 224.

with eyes, but with my whole Body, a grave, calm, noble Form in White. He said, or breathed, this phrase, " Ephphatha is good, but Amen is better still." I went away with this saying in my mind for long before I understood its force. At last in Chancel too it came to me that in The Mysteries ' Be opened,' ' Be Made Clear ' is not so Churchlike or so happy for a Xtian mind as ' So it is,' ' So let it be.' ' Knowledge ' in this Portal of the Church Universal, Life, is not so desirable as ' Acquiescence.' " He describes his secluded existence, and then continues, " Remember I do not pretend to holier life than other Men. Far, very far from that. God be merciful to me a grievous sinner. But for Seventeen Years I have fought the Battle of the Church in this Corner with a single human Succour. The Clergy around me—the wretched Heretics, the spawn of that miscreant John Wesley—the Rich and potent Landlords—all these have assailed me, and I have scourged and beaten them all continually. My sole Reliance has been on the young Men in white Garments whom I can well-nigh see, and they have conquered for me ' a Host of Men.' Once Sir J. Buller tried to take from me my Holy Well and a piece of ground. I had but £27 on Earth, for I am poor, but with one only Collect said nightly at the Altar I encountered the wealthy Baronet, Lord of the neighbouring Soil, and I did thrash him well. The Jury gave me an immediate verdict, and Sir Ahab paid into Court £1370, his own costs and mine. I laid the foundation stone of this Vicarage with but £40 in my possession and with the help of my dear Wife's Portion, I have built it well.

" And now enough of myself. Solitude makes men Self-praisers, and a Bemooster Herr, as the Germans call lonely Readers, a Mossy Vicar, likes to talk about his own importance."[1]

How clearly these simple statements, written only for the eyes of a friend, reveal the development of

---

[1] " Life and Letters," p. 228.

Hawker's character. Like many other mystics, he has set out on a course of training by means of which he may grow more closely in touch with the spiritual world, and from the exercise of the mystic's medium, Contemplation, is brought to fuller realisation of the activities of Love. It is the keynote of the two visions, though the details may appear trivial or superficial, for St. Lucy, the subject of the first, was one who sacrificed life itself for Love, and in the second the poet learns that " Knowledge . . . is not so desirable as Acquiescence "—trust founded in Love. The true mystic's aim is not to know, but to grow in Love. Yet Hawker's old weakness is still present ; self still pushes itself to the front, though its activities are different. Love of fame has become love of power, and he has allowed extravagant superstitions such as belief in the efficacy of charms and exorcism to take root in his mind. True, he uses his " supernatural " weapons at first for the good of the Church, but it is easy to detect the ring of delight at getting his own way, when he speaks of those who had opposed him.

From a literary point of view the correspondence with Dickens, then editor of " Household Words," was of more importance. In November Hawker tells his brother : " I am to contribute to ' Household Words ' and cannot send MSS. too often. There is also in the last No. of Chambers' Edinburgh Journal a paper in eulogy of the Vicar of Morwenstow, written by Hurton, the Author of ' From Leith to Lapland.' I am in receipt, too, of daily letters of encouragement to write and of praise. But too late—too late."[1] His articles to " Notes and Queries " grow few and far between, not because he feels unable to write, but because, to quote his own words, " I discovered that the Editor, after professing impartiality, was a Boundless Protestant, and that he thought fit to keep MSS. which I sent to N. and Q. for some large

[1] " Life and Letters," p. 249.

work on Folklore of his own, and what did go into his paper was curtailed."[1]

In the next year he had a recurrence of illness. He writes in 1856, " Once three years agone, I lost consciousness of passing events for . . . *nearly six weeks* ! ! and the only medical opinion was pressure of *thought*."[2] But in spite of a declaration in a letter that " my thoughts go down in MS. of which I have drawers full. But I print no more,"[3] he contributed to "Household Words" two prose articles, " The Gauger's Pocket "[4] and " The Light of Other Days,"[5] and to " Willis's Current Notes," his revised version of the old ballad, " Arscott of Tetcott."[6] The two sketches of Cornish smuggling life mark his first attempt to write according to the public taste, and do not betray the eccentric ideas which appear in his other writings at this time. Even his poetry is disfigured by them, for the poem on the Crimean War, called "Baal-Zephon," and dated November 14th, 1854, because, Hawker wrote, "it was the day of the great Storm in the Black Sea when the vessels were lost, and I wrote on that event,"[7] is unintelligible in parts without some knowledge of Hawker's superstitious beliefs on demons and charms. Who would imagine that he " of course referred to the Electric Telegraph "[8] in the verse

> Lords of the vassal air, the lightning-tongue,
> The harnessed fires with footsteps like the storm !
> Where is your vaunt, and what your strength among
> Those riders of the cloud, with battle warm ?

His only other appearance in print was in " Notes and Queries," to which he contributed remarks on the " Bosses in Morwenstow Church," and on the " Sigil

1 " Life and Letters," p. 250.
2 *Ibid.*, p. 283.
3 Baring-Gould, p. 245.
4 " Household Words," Vol. VI., p. 515.
5 *Ibid.*, Vol. VIII., p. 305.
6 Willis's " Current Notes," p. 97—8.
7 " Cornish Ballads," p. 144.
8 " Life and Letters," p. 256.

of Solomon,"[1] subjects which recur with monotonous frequency during the next few years.

In 1855 Hawker made another true friend. An appeal which he issued for money to restore the roof of the Church came to the notice of a Mrs. Watson, then living at Budleigh Salterton. She sent a donation, which Hawker acknowledged with gratitude, and the correspondence thus begun lasted with hardly a break in the weekly letters for fifteen years. Though they never met each other, Hawker saw in her someone who cared for what he had most at heart, and she came into his life just when he needed a sympathetic friend. His wife was over seventy, and losing sight and strength, and he felt he could not take all his troubles to her as he had been wont to do. To Mrs. Watson he unburdened his soul, and she responded nobly, not only encouraging him by her friendship, but helping him also in a practical way by adding a sum of money annually to his income. Without her Hawker's old age might have been a tragedy indeed ; as it is, the years 1855—1860 are less melancholy than the five preceding ones.

But we must return to Hawker's appeal for funds, for it is too characteristic to be omitted. There is no need to give the details, for the pamphlet tells its own story, and shows, too, the character of its writer. It is headed by a text, and runs as follows :—" The Roof of Morwenstow Church is covered with Shingle instead of Slate, i.e., with Tiles of Wood—the material of the Ark, and of the Cross, that Death-bed of our Blessed Lord. This kind of covering was the wise and careful choice of our Fore-fathers to baffle the Tempests of ' the Severn Sea.' In the presence of the Atlantic, and lifted full 400 feet on a Cliff above the Shore, this Wooden Roof had borne the Brunt of the Seasons and the Winds, for long generations, at a far less cost of Repair, and with much slighter injury from annual Storms than any *slated* Church in the Deanery of

[6] " Notes and Queries," X., p. 123.

Trigg Major, or on the North Coast of Cornwall. Now, the Vicar is proud of this Shingle Roof, and the hostile farmers have found it out. It has been their muttered threat and their shameless avowal that ' they would punish the Vicar by destroying his favourite Roof.' Since the late decision in the House of Lords, they have laid a crafty and malignant scheme to cover the Church like a Cattle Shed or a barn ; and at the last Vestry, the paltry Penny in the Pound for the usual yearly repair, was refused under the insidious cry of ' No Slate, no Rate.' Every effort to assuage their ferocity has been in vain. The Church Rate has been lowered during the present Incumbency from £32 a year to £16. The outlay of the Vicar, for the future good of his Parish, has been unlimited, and it has exhausted all his means. He is very, very loath that the noble Roof should fall a sacrifice, and that to the Schismatic hatred of mere Rack-Renters with no interest in the Church, and no permanence in the Scene. It has occurred to him that an appeal to his Guests and Friends, for their aidance in this final endeavour to sustain Morwenstow Church may not be utterly in vain. A Part of the Roof of the Southern Aisle has lately been renewed, and it is proposed to continue the restoration of the rest. Every Shilling in Oblation, *ad honorem Dei*, shall be made known, with the Donor's name ; and will be rigidly accounted for by the Vicar himself.

" The Vicar leads the List with £10."[1]

Hawker's evil spirit, the demon of vanity, was no easy one to cast out, but his very weaknesses make him the more human. Not to him can we apply the word " saintly," as we may to George Herbert or Keble, but he has an appeal which is far wider than theirs, because his " palpable imperfections " bring him down to the level of ordinary men. The fighting spirit was both his weakness and his strength : by this

---

[1] " Life and Letters, p. 150.

he stirred his parishioners to rebellion, by this he conquered the evil in himself.

The renewed vitality apparent in this episode is shown also in literary work. He contributed to " Willis's Current Notes,"[1] a poem and some half-dozen articles which he evidently considered of value as he speaks of wishing to fix them " in type for future days." Probably what he most desired to preserve did not appear in print, for " Willis's Current Notes " do not contain any article on " Numyne," although Hawker acknowledges the return of his MS. " well-thumbed by someone,"[2] and writes to the Rev. William West, " How I wish for some Publication which would give me free access to its columns, and thro' which I could pour out a Mass of MSS. notes and Thoughts inscribed in my solitude of 20 years here by the Sea. I have discovered among other Things a new and another Element : The Atmosphere of God and Angels. I have named it ' Numyne.' Remember I claim the Word."[3]

Those articles which were accepted contain little of interest except to an antiquarian. Hawker repeats his views on churchyards, the posture of the buried dead, the grotesque in Church architecture, and the symbolic hand, and deals with such other themes as the bronze galley at Sebastopol. From these it is only too clear that his thought has become stagnant, and, unless its current is quickened by some new influence, or its surface rippled by little breezes of inspiration, it will show no signs of life. What other result could be expected from a situation such as he describes in June 1855. " The misery with me is that here I have no Books. Not one Library exists on the total Tamarside. I can't afford to buy, so my ' Summa ' and meditation in my Chancel are the sole sources of thought that I possess."[4] And though there were breaks in his

1 " Willis's Current Notes," pp. 31, 35, 42, 45, 47, 90, 92, 93.
2 " Life and Letters," p. 255.
3 *Ibid.*, p. 254.
4 *Ibid.*, p. 258.

monotonous existence, for he writes in October of having " had the house very full lately,"[1] this state of affairs cannot have been conducive to literary work.

Towards the end of 1855 he hoped to publish " ane litel beuk of say 100 pages of my best Ballads,"[2] as he wrote to Mr. Maskell. Unfortunately he was unable to do so owing to lack of money, and the depression resulting from this seems to have prevented any more literary work till August 1856. In that month he writes of " a visit from a Mr. Blight, Son of a Schoolmaster in Penzance, an Artist. He has already published a Vol. containing the Antiquities, (Crosses, etc.) of West Cornwall, and he is now going to publish those of East Cornwall."[3] The subject was, of course, very near to Hawker's heart, and he contributed four of his early poems and a number of notes on the antiquities of Morwenstow Church, but there is little new material, and the only interest of the volume for us is that it shows Hawker apparently content to remain in the rut into which he has fallen, and still so anxious about the fate of his writings that he declares, " If any of these Notes are printed, they are not to be altered in a single word. And let each be identified by my Cipher."[4]

Still it is not to be wondered at that he wrote little of value during these years. In September 1857 he gives an account of his usual day. " My days are, I assure you, all working days (Sundays included). Let me recall. Breakfast over, I see my animals and Glebe, and people who come daily till eleven—then into the Parish with Mrs. H. or alone as she can or not—home —dine at one—till Three, read and write—Church again—Walk if fine—home—read and write till Ten, and after to Mrs. H. in Bed. I read till Midnight," and we are told that " he would read novel after novel to her, when her sight failed, without knowing in the

1 " Life and Letters," p. 205.
2 Ibid., p. 258.
3 Ibid., p. 263.
4 Ibid., p. 265.

least what they were about. His eye followed the print and his voice uttered the words, but his thoughts were far away."[1] In the next month he writes to the Rev. W. D. Anderson of his wife's illness, and continues, " A load like lead is never away from my ganglions, and reading, except aloud to Mrs. H., and writing I have quite given up . . . Besides all other goads there is the dull daily drop on drop that wears out the soul with low mean degrading money fears."[2] In March 1858 he gives an account of his only other method of expression besides his letters. " My own writing is of this kind. A sewn book, i.e., twelve of these sheets sewn together sermon shape without covers is laid upon my table. When a thought occurs or phrase worthy of ink I jot it down and when one MS. Book is full another is sewn and in this way many scores of such memda. books are now gathered into my drawers. Perhaps one day they may be read and printed as ' the Fragments of a broken mind.' "[3]

Broken in the sense that he lacked the constructive power to connect his scattered thoughts into a coherent whole, his mind certainly was. But it had not lost its strength. Many years before Hawker had noted " A full Brain may be desultory,"[4] and it is partly the wide range covered by his meditations which makes his note-books appear such a strange medley. Those from 1855—1860 are even more discursive than the earlier ones, for the dogmatic element is less apparent. God and Man, spirit and matter—with such subjects for thought is his mind filled ; is there any wonder that the notes often seem incongruous ? We may see how close in Hawker's mind is all creation to its Creator from such a note as the following. " The Animals were[5] the Attributes of God visibly roaming the Earth. The Lion was awful Power alive. The Bull

1 " Life and Letters," p. 302.
2 Ibid., p. 302.
3 Ibid., p. 370.
4 Unpublished.
5 i.e., before the Fall.

E

spurned the Hills [with] His strength. The Eagle Sped swiftness. The Man was the Intellectual Image manifest in ' Form of Flesh '."[1] The meditations on God, angels, demons ; on man—his attributes, customs and language ; on theology and life—all spring from an underlying unity in Hawker's mind, which makes it easy for him to pass from the deep to the trivial— from thoughts on the Trinity to notes on Red Indian customs and the quality of his own horse, Nectan. He was evidently as much interested at this time in books of travel as in religious or literary writings, for he writes notes on the Chinese, Japanese, Indians, Negroes, and Indians of both North and South America, and the only literary works he seems to have read are essays by Coleridge and De Quincey, Masson's Life of Milton and an Arthurian romance. As he knows the psychology of his parishioners through and through, he seeks further material by studying what he can learn of foreign races. His mind is still alert, though not creative.

Yet this year, 1858, is remarkable for a reawakening of the spirit of poetry within him. In addition to writing the " Lines of Dedication to H.R.H. the Prince of Wales " for Mr. Blight's " Ancient Crosses and other Antiquities in East and South Cornwall," he sent four poems to " The Lamp." Three are renderings of ancient legends of the Church, but the fourth is one of the poet's most individual songs, and full of mystic joy and peace. Invoking " Miriam : Star of the Sea," he cries,

> My Morning Star ! the shades of sorrow banish ;
>   Kindle me hope and bravery in my soul.
> Let care's dark shadows from my spirit vanish,
>   As mountain-clouds before the Orient roll !
>
> .   .   .   .
>
> Fear's idle dream, and Hope's all-shadowy pleasure—
>   Sorrow and joy, that vain and idle be—

[1] Unpublished.

The deep hath swallowed up the golden treasure :
Soothe thou the tempest, and subdue the sea.

. . . .

Thou Star of Peace ! Glory and gladness blending,
  Here as we lowly kneel, look love on high ;
Hail, blessed orb ! alive with light descending,
  A lamp to lead us to our native sky ! [1]

Unfortunately this burst of song is not sustained, and
there is little to record for the next five years. In 1859
he writes, " Sometimes I say, if I could but be set
down now with youth and health upon a lowly
vantage ground, the World should hear of me. But
still Time and the Hour would again whiten the hair
and paralyze the hand,"[2] and all he produces is a short
poem to hail the appearance of Tennyson's " Idylls
of the King." In 1860 we find him speculating on the
purpose of his life,[3] and writing two poems on the
mystery of the Incarnation, the one, " Aishah
Schechinah," inspired by Catholic dogma, the other,
" King Arthur's Waeshael," by Christmas tradition
in Cornwall. In the next year the appearance of the
comet proved a source of inspiration, for he wrote
that he intended to compose " Seven Stanzas in the
measure of my lines on the ' Lost President ' "[4] on
the subject. But the completed poem had a disheart-
ening reception. " There seems to be no shadow of
sympathy between the men of my generation and
myself," he writes. " If I print anything in prose or
verse no one cares even to read it. No one ever notices
the thoughts or language—neither the mower nor he
that gathereth the sheaves. Only regard my lines on
the Comet. They were tabooed by ' The Times,' no
literary journal would admit them, the Editor of the
' Oriental Budget ' rejected them because His paper
' only admitted *literary* compositions.' " However the

[1] " Cornish Ballads," p. 155.
[2] " Life and Letters," p. 315.
[3] *V.* " Life and Letters," p. 327.
[4] " Life and Letters," p. 343.

E 2

letter ends on a more cheerful note. " I still cling to
'Notes and Queries'—indeed, badly as the staff have
behaved to me, Thoms does admit my MSS., and
under different Signatures I send him Prose and
Verse."[1] The prose is negligible, but the verse is re-
presented by the rousing ballad, " Sir Beville—The
Gate-Song of Stowe," a poem as full of vigour as the
Trelawny Ballad of his youth.

But in this case he had an incentive beyond his own
desire to write. " A new feature in my history has
just set in," he tells us. " Young Ladies have betaken
themselves to the office of setting to music (their own)
my words. Hence the 'Trelawny Ballad,' and the
'Cornish Mother's Wail,' by a Miss Clare, a friend of
the Kennaways. A Miss Harris of Hayne invents a
tune and fixes a difficult metre, Moore's Song, 'She
is far from the land where her young hero sleeps.'
Thus has she extorted from me a Theme of the Caval-
iers called 'Sir Beville.' But all this fails to fulfil a
single exigency of my realities, i.e., one Golden Coin.
I have long adopted Old Johnson's dogma that he is
a fool who writes for any motive but payment."[2] He
writes more fully on this theme early in 1862—" With
regard to the Book of Days, Mr. Godwin a friend of
Robert Chambers sent it to me gratuitously and suggested my contributing to it. If I am to be paid for it
I will, but no other motive has power to move me to
lift a pen for such unavailing vanities as name or
Fame. For all such impulses my answer is 'Too late,
too late.' There is a great deal of good sense in your
reasoning that praise might have spoilt me and flattery
would have made me proud. But if I could have
realized some money while my Wife could have shared
it with me, if I could have earned what would have
made her more comfortable, it would have given me
a not unworthy pride and much consolation."[3] Praise

---

[1] " Life and Letters," p. 277.
[2] *Ibid.*, p. 268.
[3] *Ibid.*, p. 355.

might indeed have turned his head, but it was not lack of appreciation alone which made him cease to write poetry, and praise might on the other hand have stimulated him to further effort. As it is, though three of his early poems appeared in Chambers' " Book of Days," the only new poem of this year was called forth by a terrible wreck—that of the " Bencoolen " in October 1862. Hawker thought that the men of Bude had failed in their duty, and all the passion of his Celtic temperament breathes through the grim irony of " A Croon on Hennacliff."

> " Cawk ! cawk ! " then said the raven,
> " I am fourscore years and ten :
> Yet never in Bude Haven
>   Did I croak for rescued men—
> They will save the Captain's girdle,
>   And shirt, if shirt there be :
> But leave their blood to curdle
>   For my old dame and me." [1]

There are no signs here of weakness or lack of vitality.

But the next year, 1863, brought to Hawker the greatest sorrow of his life. In February his wife died. Though now eighty years of age, and blind, she had been his constant companion to the end, " full of cheerfulness and geniality, laughing over her husband's jokes, and drawing him out with a subtle skill to show himself to his best advantage. In his fits of depression she was invaluable to him, always at his side, encouraging him and directing his thoughts to pleasant topics."[2] Accustomed to turn to her at every difficulty for sympathy and encouragement, and to lean on her advice, he felt himself now left to battle single-handed against the evils of this mortal life. For a time he gave way to a mood of utter depression. " My desolate self," he writes, " to whom the end of all things is now so near, that it cannot matter much where I live and how the fragment of my days may

---

[1] " Cornish Ballads," p. 170.
[2] Baring-Gould, p. 183.

fall to dust. I am indeed crushed. Every thought and feeling and plan have been so blended and fastened on Her that I am like a man without a hope or fear."[1]

As time passed, however, he grew more resigned, and following the suggestion of one of his friends began to work on a poem. Some years before he had said, " If I can but fix my mind upon a given subject, it is a relief to me at all times to compose—God gave me, I think, the power as a solace,"[2] and as his need of such was now greater than ever before, so the result must always be considered his highest achievement. Professor Saintsbury's statement[3] that he was " *induced* " to write the poem gives a wrong impression. He had had the desire to write on King Arthur since his youth, and his mind was full of material on the subject ; the " inducement " of his friends was merely the spur which his flagging will needed to bring it " to the sticking-point." Yet again we have to regret " a broken purpose," for Hawker finished only one chant of the five he had planned on the subject of " The Quest of the Sangraal."

Although the poem is unfinished, however, the revelation of its author given by the one chant leaves but little to be supplied by the shadowy four. Into " The Quest of the Sangraal " Hawker put all his heart, his mind, his soul, his strength. It is the mature expression of his " all of love," it holds imbedded in itself the thoughts of years of solitude, and with no uncertain voice it speaks of the Vision granted to the soul of the mystic.

At a first glance we notice the poet's love of Cornish scenery, of romantic legend, and of the teaching of the Catholic Church, and thus find entwined to form a thing of beauty the three strands which ran through all the work of his youth—nature—the past—religion. We are next struck by the appearance of such a phrase

---

[1] " Life and Letters," p. 408.
[2] " Life and Letters," p. 306.
[3] Camb. Hist. of Eng. Lit., vol. XII., p. 134.

as " the cone of space " and its attendant note, but it is soon clear that Hawker is making this poem a storehouse of all the grain, and incidentally some of the chaff, which he has collected during his years of meditation. It holds all his philosophy and all his theories. Hawker, however, was too keenly conscious of his own personality to be content with this objective method of presentation, and though the poem is conceived as an epic, we find the poet himself speaking through the mouth of Arthur.

> I have no son, no daughter of my loins,
> To breathe, 'mid future men, their father's name :
> My blood will perish when these veins are dry ;
> Yet I am fain some deeds of mine should live—
> I would not be forgotten in this land :
> I yearn that men I know not, men unborn,
> Should find, amid these fields, King Arthur's fame !
> Here let them say, by proud Dundagel's walls—
> " They brought the Sangraal back by his command,
> They touched these rugged rocks with hues of God : "
> So shall my name have worship, and my land.[1]

Though the poet is still writing with the thought of posterity in his mind the desire for personal fame has been commuted to something finer—a desire to further the glory of God. But is Hawker writing subjectively in these few lines only ? Those in which Arthur speaks of the loneliness of his life express Hawker's own feelings in his bereavement, and as true for him as for Arthur are the words,

> Therefore I tarry by the cruel sea,
> To hear at eve the treacherous mermaid's song,
> And watch the wallowing monsters of the wave,—
> 'Mid all things fierce, and wild, and strange, alone ![2]

If then, Arthur stands for the poet himself, much more of the poem must be autobiographical. What is the quest he cannot follow ? What is the meaning of the

[1] " Cornish Ballads," p. 186.
[2] *Ibid.*, p. 185.

words

> to win and wear the starry Sangraal,
> The link that binds to God a lonely land ?

The answer lies in the motto given to the knight who is destined to achieve the quest.

> I thirst ! O Jesu ! let me drink and die !

The self, forgotten in the overpowering desire of Love, reaches its consummation in union with the Divine. But if the poet has had the vision of the goal of the mystic's journey, what has held him back from completing the journey himself ? Was it not the conviction that he was called to be " a shepherd of souls," and so expended his energy on the practical every-day duties of the parish priest ? Moreover, in the England of his day there was work to be done in argument.

> Would that my arm went with you, like my heart,
> But the true shepherd must not shun the fold :
> For in this flock are crouching grievous wolves
> And chief among them all, my own false kin.[1]

From this point the whole poem unfolds as an allegory of life in England in the nineteenth century. The king's first speech had suggested this :—

> in vain our land
> Of noble name, high deed and famous men ;
> Vain the proud homage of our thrall, the sea,
> If we be shorn of God.   Ah ! loathsome shame !
> To hurl in battle for the pride of arms :
> To ride in native tournay, foreign war :
> To count the stars ; to ponder pictured runes,
> And grasp great knowledge, as the demons do,
> If we be shorn of God.[2]

Now all falls into place. The knights, " soldiers of the rock and ring," are the Church militant here on earth, the Church founded on a rock, the members bound by

[1] " Cornish Ballads," p. 185.
[2] *Ibid.*, p. 177.

a sacrament in which " two worlds of life and glory blend." In a world of materialism,

> Too much athirst for fame, too fond of blood ;
> And all for earth, for shadows, and the dream
> To glean an echo from the winds of song ! [1]

they give themselves up to a single-hearted quest of the Divine. In their different spheres of activity their wanderings are typical of the varying fortunes of Christian men, and thus in this poem Hawker appears to us in his full stature. He has forged through times of doubt and depression to a position from which he can speak to his own generation with the " trumpet of a prophecy," and his message, though in his own time men ignored it, is one which has triumphed over such treatment for nearly two thousand years, and which can never grow old, for it holds the secret of Life. He looked at the problems of his time from a standpoint outside his own century, but it was not with the limited vision of a mediæval monk, but with the widened outlook of one who had grasped in some measure the values of eternity.

The growth of the poem can be traced from the letters of this year, but in August another misfortune befell Hawker. A fire broke out in the Vicarage, and, though Hawker's own account gives no hint that it was as disastrous to his belongings as Mr. Baring-Gould suggests, it was not without effect on his nerves. " I am far more shaken," he writes, " than you would imagine from having to gather together papers and scattered things that I had not the courage to look at since February."[2] With great difficulty and spurred on only by his determination, he finished the first chant by the end of the year. Then followed a nervous breakdown, the natural consequence of another period of worry and intense depression, while a succession of external events also played their part in his collapse. Among these two of the chief were another ship-

[1] " Cornish Ballads," p. 186.
[2] " Life and Letters," p. 426.

wreck, that of the " Margaret Quayle," and the death
of Thackeray, but no doubt his loneliness was the outstanding factor.

It was fortunate that a new interest was to come
into his life. In October another family had come to
live in his parish, and in Mr. Valentine, Vicar of
Whixley in Yorkshire, Hawker found a friend, and to
his two little girls we owe Hawker's next two poems,
birthday verses for Eva and Matilda Valentine. Yet,
poems to children as they are, they show clearly the
ache at the poet's heart as he writes of love and marriage, and lines found among his MSS. dated August
12th, 1864, show the direction of his thoughts.

> Night falls ! the dreary Shadows creep
> Between the Mountains and the deep :
> The sunset rustles o'er the sky,
> While here I breathe my Syrian Sigh !
>
> All dark ! but gloomier from the light
> Just faded from my yearning Sight :
> The violet eyes !   The violet eyes !
> That gleam'd, a glimpse of Paradise !
>
> Ah ! awful hills ! ah ! shuddering Wave !
> A living Death : a ready grave :
> One only Star to soothe the Scene—
> The gleaming Brow of dear Pauline ! [1]

Who was this Pauline who has made so deep an impression on the poet ? She was a Miss Kuczynski,
governess to Mr. Valentine's children, and described
by Hawker when he first met her as " a very un-
pretending old-fashioned young lady of 21 or 2."[2]
Her first impressions of Hawker appear in the following letter written in January 1864. " New Year's Day
afternoon and evening I spent with Mr. V. and the
children at the Vicar's. Mr. Hawker took me and the
children to *his* cliff—his Glebe land lies on the Cliffs
chiefly—a little way down one called Vicarage cliff he

---

[1] " Cornish Ballads," p. 313.
[2] " Life and Letters," p. 476.

has made out of the hull of one of the vessels wrecked on Morwenstow rocks a hut. There we sat an hour as snug as possible, with the most splendid panorama of sky, sea and rock before us and Mr. Hawker telling me most interesting accounts of wrecks off this immediate Coast—once he buried 9 poor Sailors whose corpses had been washed up on to the beach. He is a most interesting old gentleman. Fortunately we get on well— where he takes he's charming, where he doesn't he's the other thing. He has lived a life made up of eccentricities."[1] She then describes the disparity of age between his first wife and himself, little imagining that within a year he would have added to his eccentricities by taking herself as his second wife, in spite of the forty years which lay between their ages.

The marriage proved an entirely happy one, in spite of all the arguments against it which were advanced by Miss Kuczynski's relations. Its effect on Hawker's powers as a writer was most marked, for the years 1865—67 contain most of his prose work. The death of Cardinal Wiseman on February 14th, 1865 called forth the poem " Ichabod," and in March he began a series of contributions to " All the Year Round." As his motive was mainly to increase his income, he chose the literary form most acceptable to magazines, and wrote a number of romantic accounts of events or characters connected with Morwenstow. The form is different, but the inspiration is the same as in his earliest poems, and the only characteristic in them which we have not met before is that sense of fun and gift of humorous anecdote which his friends have recorded in their descriptions of his personality. But after a time he grew disheartened at the way his work was received. A letter of June, 1865, gives his chief troubles. " The truth is unless I could create Readers with Taste and Imagination I cannot expect to be understood or appreciated. Hence the taste for the trite meagre low writing of the present day. But I am

[1] " Life and Letters," p. 444.

weary of it all. I am ready to write my fingers off to get pay, but I cannot alter my whole mind. Wills has inserted another article ' Black John,' but cut out all my best parts and worse he has put in some trash of his own as mine and made me talk nonsense in the last paragraph. No one ever was treated as I am on all hands. I only hope my load of troubles will not weigh down the bright spirits of my poor dear Pauline. She has brought me health and happiness and when I hear her singing like a bird it breaks me down."[1]

On November 27th, 1865, another burden—though a joyful one—was added to the load which Hawker already carried, for a daughter was born to them. His poetry has already shown his love of children and his regret at having none of his own, but his delight at the birth of Morwenna Pauline, as he christened her, was tempered by his sense of responsibility when he considered the provision for her future. He writes, " A human life begun in my house, and that will be prolonged into the far depths of Eternity is an awful joy. I cannot help picturing my Baby at the future age of 10 and 20 years encountering it may be the trials and the anguish of a mortal existence and closing life at the last with remembrance of sorrow and pain. Yet she may by God's marvellous mercy do well and find friends as her Father has done and pass away from this earth to stand and minister before God in Heaven." He longed greatly for a son, but his desire was not granted, for though two more children were born, they were both girls.

All his life Hawker had been more or less harassed by lack of money, and during the last nine years of his life his troubles grew more acute. His letters become more and more melancholy as he sees his expenses increasing, and feels his energy growing less. We learn from a letter written in February 1866 that his net income was about £165, and in October he tried another

---

[1] " Life and Letters," p. 522.
[2] *Ibid.*, p. 530.

method of raising money by advertising for " Two or Three Pupils from the age of 14 to 17 years to be prepared for the Universities or otherwise."[1] It was evidently a time of renewed mental activity : " I intend to work hard this Winter at MS. and reading,"[2] he writes, and later wishes he " could go on with the 'Quest.' "[3] But gloom falls upon him again, as he continues, in characteristic fashion, " a Man with a Millstone round his neck in the shape of an adverse Banker's Balance, whose shadow like that of an Eastern Prince will never be less is enough to plunge any Man's Soul into the Sea. The curse of all Writers has always been upon me. All other gifts if you seek them without stint, but neither Silver nor Gold. This of yore I did not heed, but now another thought comes from the Faces around me and I shudder as I look."[4] This cry is reiterated again and again. The edition of his collected poems published in 1868 under the title " Cornish Ballads and other Poems, including a Second Edition of the First Chant of the Quest," " is a failure, and I acquiesce in my usual doom,"[5] he writes, and similar words record the fate in 1870 of " a prose volume of reprints," with " the name of ' Footprints of the Former Men in Far Cornwall.' "[6]

It is a relief to turn from the laments which fill the letters of Hawker's old age to picture scenes which must have shed rays of brightness through the sombre melancholy which so often closed round him. He was not entirely cut off from visitors, and their descriptions show him in a better light than his own morbid confessions. He did not look like a nervous wreck. " One rarely looks upon a finer man than he was then, with his venerable silver hair and mighty chest and shoulders,"[7] says one, and another writes in 1874, " I

1 " Life and Letters," p. 534.
2 *Ibid.*, p. 548.
3 *Ibid.*, p. 546.
4 *Ibid.*, p. 558.
5 *Ibid.*, p. 580.
6 *Ibid.*, p. 588.
7 Mr. Spender, editor of *W. Morning News.* " Life and Letters," p. 592.

was very struck at his personal appearance . . . His
hair was white and long—clean-shaved face—with
bright rosy cheeks."[1] He was a delightful host, not
only to his friends, but to chance visitors. One of
these, after describing how Hawker refreshed him
with " excellent but rather strong beer," continues,
" He took us round the Parsonage grounds and with
great pride showed us many figure-heads, etc., of
derelict ships, wrecked just below his house, and he
told us of the drowned sailors whom he had buried.
I thought that, if the ships had to be wrecked, and
the men drowned, he was very pleased that the calam-
ities should occur near Morwenstow ! Then he showed
us the Church, and gave us much learned information
thereon."[2] Hawker did not brood over the ship-wrecks
as morbidly as letters written under the stress of
anxiety would lead us to believe. Another glimpse of
him is given by one who as a boy felt the charm of his
personality. Hawker " gave him permission to look
through the wonderful old books in the parsonage
library. None knew so well, nor could relate so delight-
fully as he, the exquisite legends of the ' Morte
d'Arthur,' Tristram and Isolde, Guinevere and Lancelot, Merlin and Vivien, Sir Kay the Seneschal, Sir
Galahad and the Sangraal—how full of life each of
these became under the magic of his vivid story-tell-
ing ! "[3]

He had, too, the satisfaction of knowing that some
of his work had prospered. Matthew Arnold's younger
brother, the Rev. E. P. Arnold, inspected Hawker's
church school and reported upon it. " I cannot help
congratulating the Vicar, of whose uphill labours to
support a school in this remote district I have been
witness for so many years, that he has at last succeeded
in getting this substantial and well-filled school

---

[1] " Life and Letters," p. 617.

[2] *Ibid.*, p. 607.

[3] Mr. J. Harman Ashley, editor of *Insurance Advocate* (Philadelphia
and New York). *Ibid.*, Preface, p. xv., note.

erected, and that it is now at work under a Certifi-
cated Master, with every prospect of success."[1]

We must keep these cheerful episodes in mind
while we consider the writings of Hawker's old age.
Five poems, only, mark the years from 1870—1875,
for " I must give up competition with the writers of
these days," he tells Mr. Godwin, " and confine myself to newspapers for gratuitous pieces. As soon as my
letter-bag ceases to cut me down daily like a blow
I will think of your suggestion and try to undertake
another ' Quest.' "[2] Though he was never able to carry
this into effect, the poem on the loss of " H.M.S.
Captain," and " The Carol of the Pruss," show his
never-failing interest in topical events. There is no
weakening in his powers in the poem which shows his
insight into the spirit of Prussia.

> Starve ! starve them all, till through the skin
> You may count each hungry bone :
> Tap ! tap their veins till the blood runs thin
> And their sinful flesh is gone ;
> While life is strong in the German sky,
> What matters it who beside may die !

But the letters show him overwhelmed by anxiety.
" My House," he writes, " is thick with sorrows hard
and heavy as the Nether Millstone to bear. My poor
dear Wife a chronic and crippled sufferer from rheu-
matic gout—my children, it is true, bright and health-
ful, but their future ! God help them—what I cannot
bear to look on. And I myself a living death."[3]

In addition to his personal worries, he was trying to
collect money for a second restoration of his beloved
church, and turned a visit to London, which he and
Mrs. Hawker had taken in order to seek medical advice, to good account by earning money for this
purpose by his sermons. But though Hawker was re-

---

[1] " Life and Letters," p. 619.
[2] Ibid., p. 590.
[3] Ibid., p. 598.

assured by the doctor's opinion of his health, he was
cast to the depths by his reception by the London
clergy. " Everything has gone wrong," he writes to
Mr. Godwin, " and I attribute a great deal to your
absence from London. No one to advise me, none to
help. Dr. F. G. Lee has behaved, however, most kind-
ly. He sent me Notes of Introduction to White, St.
Barnabas, Pimlico, and to Stuart, Munster Square.
The former was denied to me when I called, although
confessedly at home, and in reply to a Note from me
inclosing one from Lee he sent me a flat refusal. He
wanted all his Offertories for himself. Liddell of St.
Paul's, Knightsbridge, refused for the same reason.
Stuart, whom I saw when I called, snubbed me.
Compton of All Saints, Margaret Street, has not re-
plied to a Note from me inclosing one of request
from T. ' Doctor, The Thanes fly from me.' I have
preached for Morwenstow once only and that at
Evensong. This was a great success. ' Splendid—
lovely — most eloquent — original ' — these were the
epithets among some of the 1500 people present. The
average offertory in that church for 1872–3 had been
under £5. They gave me £26 18/- and Westall the
Curate wrote me a few days after to say that he could
not express how I had ' delighted and edified his
people and they had talked of nothing else since but
the Sermon : ' he thanked me also for what I had
taught him. This Sermon, which proves that I could
have preached if I had been allowed, I shall write
down from memory for Pauline and the Children. I
have sent a copy of the Ballads to Longfellow and
asked if he can get the Book printed in America since
England will not have it. I do wish I could get the
copies out of Parker's hands so as to print a new
Edition with added Poems left out in the last. You
will be sorry to hear that we go down to-morrow week
the 5th May with my poor dear Wife hardly a shade
better. I am nearly frenzied with the failure of this
bitter and costly effort. My resources too are exhausted

and my Normal State of Misery from this cause is deeply increased.Without some succour the results must at no distant time be fatal."[1]

Lack of money was not Hawker's only source of worry ; he was troubled by various questions which at this time were agitating the Church of England. He was much perturbed by the Public Worship Regulation Bill, and composed an epigram on the doubtful baptism of Archbishop Tait. What was probably his last poem was a song of praise at " Manning's Elevation to the Cardinalate," and a letter containing a question on this ceremony shows that he had not given up hope of continuing the " Quest," for evidently the second chant was to begin

$$\text{Ho! for the Sangraal! once again I} \begin{cases} \text{smite} \\ \text{cleave} \end{cases}$$
The dream of Echo with a Shout of Song.

But he was to write no more and the end was not far off. In April he decided to take his family on a holiday to visit his brother at Plymouth, but, finding on their arrival that the latter was seriously ill, they had to remain in lodgings. Hawker had given his curate the use of the Vicarage, so they could not return to Morwenstow, though he longed intensely to do so. He had had a presentiment that he would die away from it, for, it is recorded, " on the Sunday previous to his departure he preached a farewell sermon to his parishioners at Morwenstow who were so moved by it that after the service they crowded round him in tears."[2] His presentiment was only too true, for, after failing visibly both in body and mind, he became suddenly worse, and on August 15th he died.

Much has been written on the fact that a few hours before he died Mrs. Hawker sent for a priest of the Roman Catholic Church, and that her husband was received into that faith. Mrs. Hawker had learnt all she knew of the Catholic faith from her husband and was

[1] " Life and Letters," pp. 613, 614.
[2] *Ibid.*, p. 632.

F

fully convinced that she was carrying out his wishes.
There is no doubt that Hawker, led by his reading and
his imagination, did practically hold the Roman interpretation of the Catholic Faith on some points of
doctrine. His view of the Virgin Mary is a case in
point. His mind dwells on her because she was the
human means by which God became Man, and as
mystic he is ever searching with awe and wonder into
the meaning of the Incarnation. But much that was
not primarily religious goes also to make up his attitude. The great sorrow of his early life—" I have no
son, no daughter of my fame To breathe 'mid future
hearts their father's name "[1]—leads him to think of
her as the type of motherhood, and as time passes,
a desire for which he could find no expression in his
own life, finds satisfaction in the ideal of the Mother
and her Babe, and love from its very idealism passes
into worship. But, though he was close to Roman
thought, it must ever be a matter of conjecture
whether he would have taken the final step on his own
initiative. Apparently he did not subscribe to many of
the practices and claims of Rome, and, though he saw
only too clearly the faults of the English Church, she
was to him even as late as 1874, "our dear old church,"
and when his mind was whole he saw equally clearly
the faults of Rome. The notes he made were in the
nature of arguments for and against statements of
doctrine, rather than simple statements of belief. We
cannot doubt that he never saw his path clear. It was
his misfortune to live during a time of suspicion and
distrust, and to be judged by men who looked on
compromise as treachery. A more broad-minded and
tolerant age will see in his brother's words the best
summing-up of the situation. " I am not in a position
even to think, still less to enlarge on the views which
it is alleged my Brother held with regard to the Faith.
I never exchanged a word with him on the subject . . .
You will believe I am very heterodox, but I am of the

[2] " Cornish Ballads," p. 136.

Church of God, the great Cathedral Church of the Universe, and I do not care to dwell on my Brother's memory unless it be in connection with his own words,

> Youth, Manhood, Old Age past
> Come to thy God at last.[1]

The account given of Hawker's last hours is by Mrs. Hawker and is naturally prejudiced in favour of her own reading of his wishes, but nothing can disguise the joy of the mystic as his vision of the spiritual world grows clearer, nor alter the fact that one of his last conscious acts was to touch the mainspring of the mystic's life in the word, " Love." These are Mrs. Hawker's words. " When I told my Husband what I had done he raised himself instantly, and, seeming for the moment as if all bodily anguish was forgotten, exclaimed, ' Thank God, the Church, and Pauline.' ' Tide of Glory,' ' Tide of Joy,' the Gloria in excelsis Deo, to the end—then the Te Deum. Hitherto the Penitential Psalms had been constantly on his lips. But, on that Eve of the Assumption, the last day of his life, after he had heard that the desire of his Soul was about to be satisfied, he repeated all joyful Canticles, and again and again and again these two verses : ' What shall I render to the Lord for all that he hath rendered unto me ? I will take the Chalice of Salvation and call upon the name of the Lord.' Once he lifted his hand and pointing towards the closed door as if he saw a supernatural form, said, ' His banner over me was love.' "[2]

" What a Life mine would be if it were all written and published in a book,"[3] said Hawker himself. As we look back over its course, it seems to resolve into a series of contrasts, which yet form a perfect whole, as do the diverse colours of a ray of light. There is first before us the contrast in the man's own life ; the unfulfilled promise of his youth as we see it typified on

[1] Brit. Mus. M.S., 37, 825. Letter 12.
[2] " Life and Letters," p. 637.
[3] *Ibid.*, p 522.

F 2

the one hand in the joyous activity of his boyhood
and undergraduate days, and on the other in the sad
and ineffective labour which marked the latter part of
his life. There are the contrasts between youth and
age which he himself brought about in his two mar-
riages. There are the contrasts in his own character.
We see the virility, the decision, the steadfastness of
the man, and linked with them as a foil the excitability,
the petulance, the changeful temper of the child. We
see the practical hardheadedness of the capable man
of affairs, and side by side with it the dreaming love of
beauty of the artist. Humility and arrogance are yoke-
fellows ; faith and doubt move hand in hand. At one
time we see a wavering soul tossed hither and thither
by cross-currents and contrary winds ; at another the
mystic strong in faith pursues his course unwearied
towards the goal.

Finally, there is the contrast between Hawker's
life and the age in which he lived. In touch with the
progress of events as far as he could be through the
medium of newspapers and reviews, he was yet as far
removed from their effect as " some far-off watcher of
the skies," and his attitude was almost as detached.
It is difficult to realise that he was living through some
of the most crowded years of English history, years
in which the average citizen was so often forced to
change the focus of his vision to take in some new
thing that it left him groping and bewildered. As
Mr. Nicholson says in his study of Tennyson, the
Victorians " saw their daily lives . . . changing before
their eyes with a startling and jerky rapidity ; they
saw political power wrested from the hands of the
territorial aristocracy by the industrial middle classes
only to fall finally to the masses ; they saw local authority passing gradually from the squire and the
rector to end in an autonomous parish council ; they
saw the idea of Empire emerging from the old planta-
tion conception, through the purely geographical
phase, through a wholly emotional transition, towards

the broader aim of Commonwealth."[1] Hawker was affected by none of these. He writes in 1862, " Did you ever hear that for every 100 miles you live from London, you must reckon yourself a Century back from your own date ? We therefore, who are 250 miles off are now in the year 1610 in all that relates to agriculture and civilisation."[2] Morwenstow was outside the march of progress ; its inhabitants had no practical knowledge of new inventions, for even to-day it is still untouched by the railway, and Hawker himself had only travelled by train once before 1864. Industrial conditions were outside his ken, and all his life he was the benevolent autocrat of his parish. Apparently his only view of the colonies was as a dumping-ground for emigrants.[3] He could give no help to his generation in their practical difficulties.

But there were other problems before the Victorians and in solving them Hawker's detached position was no drawback. Mr. Nicholson continues, "They saw science and invention opening illimitable and fantastic vistas into the unknown ; they saw the very foundations of their faith and conscience cracking before the advancing billows of criticism and analysis." While they were anxious, Hawker was serene, for he saw these doubts and questions of a harassed time balanced by their real value in eternity. He could offer spiritual consolation to his age, because spirit is " a thing immortal," and therefore unaffected by time or circumstances. For the same reason he may appeal to " men unborn," for, though the transitory elements of his eccentric life merely awaken interest, he may wield influence through the enduring stuff of his work. A poet's life is not lived only for his own time, and it is in his thought and art we must look for its meaning.

1 Tennyson, p. 2.
2 " Life and Letters," p. 361.
3 V. " Life and Letters," p. 401.

CHAPTER IV.

HAWKER AS THINKER.

THE mystic is like a traveller who has climbed a hill while other way-farers plod along the road which follows all the windings of the valley below. They see not whither the road leads, but from the height he can distinguish their goal, and in the view spread before him has a vision of beauty which he feels he must try to describe to them, though he can hardly find words for the task. Even if mists float across and obscure the view before he has gazed his fill, he has something to tell the world, and though the world's laughter or neglect may dishearten him, it can never make him forget the vision or doubt the truth of its existence. If he is a sensitive man, as Hawker was, it may influence the way in which he tells his tale ; he may clothe his message in different forms in the effort to attract popular attention, but the matter remains the same. For that reason it is possible to consider Hawker's thought apart from the form in which it is expressed, for he, unlike most mystics, was acutely conscious of his audience, and tried various ways of appealing to them. With the vision before him, he began by calling to them from the top of the hill, but they took no notice of his poetry, so he came down from the heights, and hid his message like " stones broken from the rocks," knowing that his own generation would never find them, but hoping that in the future some passers-by might light on them. Under the stress of great emotion he returned to the top of the hill, and again chanted his vision, now clearer than before, to a world which ignored and misunderstood it, and then, growing old and very weary, came down and found a few people who would listen if he told them about objects which they could see on the lower slopes of the hill. But because his greatest power was his " shaping spirit of Imagination," so his truest expression was in the highest form of imaginative language, and the straightest road to an appreciation of Hawker's thought leads through his poetry. We may need his letters, notes and prose, to show the workings of his mind, or the different stages in the development of a thought, but his poetry will hold " the conclusion of the whole matter."

We have already seen what kind of soil was necessary for the seed of Hawker's imagination to spring to life. " He writes poems," one may answer, " about himself, about nature, about the past, about religion —all most popular themes, especially among writers with only a feeble glimmer of poetic imagination." But there is nothing superficial in Hawker's treatment of them, for he sees them as different manifestations of one absorbing theme, and what he was supremely interested in was Life—its opportunities, its problems and its mystery. That alone is enough to make him treat well-worn themes " with a difference," for a poet's words must carry weight, if he has once listened to the beating of the world's heart; and though some poets in their youth may think in terms of the world, may, like Shelley, " desire to awaken a noble nation from the lethargy of despair," or, like Keats, be ambitious to " do some good to the world," there are others who turn first to the individual, and who see in the personalities around them an epitome of human nature all the world over. Such poets tend to be highly self-conscious, for their chief interest is in the psychology of the individual, and they find in themselves, as well as in their neighbours, material for analysis and research. Hawker's kinship with Wordsworth is due to their view of nature, and to the desire common

to both to portray the emotions and passions of those
with whom they come in contact, but the resemblance
goes no further, for in temperament the two are poles
apart. Wordsworth made a systematic study of the
progress of his soul, while Hawker denied his imagination the expression it craved for, though at moments
of intense emotion it wrung from him, as we have
seen, cries of joy or pain. His own words show the
contrast. In " Words by the Waters," he finds his
native countryside symbolic of his own nature. He sees

> the mountain, clothed in cloud,
> The shore of tempests when the storm is loud,
> Where wild winds rush, and broken waters roll,
> And all is dark and stern, like my own wintry soul !

What has he to say of Wordsworth ? In his conversation with Tennyson in 1848, he reports, " We talked
of the sea, which he and I equally adore. But as he
told me strange to say Wordsworth cannot bear its
face. My solution was, that nursed among the still
waters with a mind as calm and equable as his lakes
the Scenery of the rough Places might be too boister-
ous for the meek man's Soul." Whether meekness was
the outstanding characteristic of Wordsworth is open
to question, but it certainly had no part in Hawker's
disposition, and it has been only too clear that his imagination, when centred on himself, became puffed up
with pride, and was the cause of that spiritual arrogance, which at one period of his life struck such a
jarring note.

Apart from this, however, his imagination had a
perfectly natural and a fruitful growth. All through
his life any one of the three sparks of inspiration may
set his poet's mind afire, but the force of their appeal
varies, and though " a threefold cord is not easily
broken," and the strands of Hawker's thought are so
closely entwined that it is often difficult to separate
them, it is possible to see three phases in his work.

[1] " Cornish Ballads," p. 125.
[2] " Life and Letters," p. 191.

In his youth and early manhood, he is interested in
life in the past, and finds material ready to his hand
in the legends which cling to many natural objects
around his home ; in his prime, he is concerned with
life in the present, and turns to nature and the Christian faith for lessons on thought and conduct ; and in
his old age his imagination is engrossed with the life
in the future towards which his religion has always
pointed. Any attempt, however, to keep the discussion of his thought within rigid lines will only result
in overlapping and repetition, for one line of thought
never stands alone. While his senses always respond
to the beauty of nature, his soul, though with a mystic's
conviction of a personal revelation, is directed by his
love of the past to find satisfaction in the dogma of the
Catholic Church. And, though for some mystics, acceptance of such would have meant a limitation of
their vision, it held for Hawker " suggestions which
are boundless."[1] He saw in the Catholic Church a
living entity, holding God's full revelation of Himself
to man, with a historic beginning in its foundations by
Christ, by its very existence a witness in the present
to the reality of spiritual things, to which all creation
in a less obvious way testified, and a herald of that life
in eternity of which he in his own consciousness was
sometimes aware. Thus all his thought revolves round
a fixed centre—the Church in which he held office, and
one of the many contrasts presented by his life is
brought about by the play of his imagination on it :
we see him now seizing with spiritual insight on some
eternal truth, now amusing himself ingeniously with
some of the extraneous matter which the Church has
acquired in her passage through the centuries. His own
character and his education lie at the root of this development, and its progress is mirrored in his poetry.

We have already noticed the light thrown on
Hawker himself by his boyish poems of 1821. He takes
a delight in describing his own emotions, especially

[1] " Life and Letters," p. 77.

those called out by domestic relations and by natural beauty, but there are signs, too, of an interest in the passions which move mankind. The fallen chieftain is a picture of one whose " proud soul " is " dark . . . with the lust of ambition,"[1] the man who died of rage is a

> dreadful page of nature's book
> . . . . . . wherein hearts might read,
> In words of fire how many a loathsome deed
> Of strange unholy darkness must have been
> Before the world could bring forth so much sin.[2]

It is all very crude and elementary, of course, but "straws show which way the wind blows," and Hawker's choice of the ballad form for his next poem, and for those in his first mature volume, was not just in youthful imitation of Scott. He used it because the ballad is in its essence the expression of the primitive but unchanging passions of men, and because his own literary education had made him aware of its fitness for his purpose.

With this step we come face to face with a problem which it is impossible to solve accurately. Hawker himself tells us that, when he was at Oxford, he devoured " a vast Number of Books," but though we cannot find out the extent of his reading, remarks in his letters help us to estimate its nature, and this we must do to realise the background of all his thought.

First and foremost in his studies came the Bible. Much later in his life he wrote that in it " there is food for the enthusiast's dream ; rhetoric for the multitude ; argument for the logical ; poetry for the imaginative ; moral definitions for the matter-of-fact individual;"[3] and before he went to Oxford the stories of David and Deborah had inspired him. His theological career only gave him a more intimate knowledge of the book which moulded his whole life. In 1864 he

---

[1] " Cornish Ballads," p. 278.
[2] *Ibid.*, p. 280.
[3] " Stones Broken from the Rocks," p. 71.

describes how in his youth he " built a kind of log hut in the wood, a mile from any house, and there read for Deacon's Orders, only going home at night, . . . and learnt St. Paul's Epistles by heart there,"[1] while a letter of 1857 adds the information, " Once I could begin the Old Testament and repeat every prophecy from Genesis to Malachi, which related to our Lord and His Gospel."[2] The same letter refers to his knowledge of the " Hebrew commentaries, called the Talmud," and from a letter of 1868 we gather that he had first studied it in a " Latin Translation . . . which belongs to Magdalen Hall Library and which Macbride allowed me to bring down to Bude and read in the Long Vacation."[3] He found more material to his liking in the writings of the early Fathers, and, from references to them in letters, must have dipped, either now or when he was in Oxford in 1845 to take his M.A., into the work of Origen, Jerome, Augustine and Ephrem Syrus. How much he knew of the writings of the great sixteenth and seventeenth century divines of the Anglican Church it is impossible to judge, but there too his knowledge was probably wide rather than deep. He was certainly keenly interested in the development of the Catholic Church, in the relation of its three branches—Greek, Roman and Anglican—to each other, and especially in the constitution of the one of which he was a member, but at this early date the work of his reason on their differences of thought was probably subordinate to that of his imagination on their historical significance.

It was at this time that life in the past called to him more forcefully than either life in the present or in the future, and he fed his imagination on " Old-World Histories." In 1857 he declares, " I have read, I think, nearly all ancient History, and of course modern also,"[4] and we may guess that his range included Josephus

1 " Life and Letters," p. 21.
2 Ibid., p. 297.
3 Ibid., p. 568.
4 Ibid., p. 301.

and Sir Thomas Malory,[1] " a very old translator of
Herodotus in quaint Shakspearian English," Dray-
ton's " Polyolbion " and his " Baron's Wars,"[2] Lin-
gard's " History of the Edwards," and Hallam's
" Middle Ages."[3] These probably attracted him more
at this time than literature pure and simple, for he
already had a close acquaintance with the work of
those who most affected his poetry—Shakespeare,
Milton, Byron, Scott and Moore,[4] and the only English poet who can be definitely placed among his
reading at Oxford is Landor. How much influence he
exerted may be gathered from Hawker's characteristic
statement in 1858, " When I was at Oxford his
Poetry was in vogue, and I read it ; but he was always
utterly void of Religious Belief, and now the end of
these things is death."[5] But, judging from the few
translations of Goethe's and Schiller's poems dated
1826, and the fact that the first Mrs. Hawker later
published translations from Görres and Oehlen-
schlager, we may assume that she led him to read
German poetry, and we can only regret her guidance.
Hawker was not the man to profit from German influence as Carlyle did. He was too closely knit in
temper to the spirit of the Folksongs, and he needed
something more bracing. We shall see the disastrous
results of his pursuit of the mediæval in German
literature after his discovery of Gretser.

It is certainly clear that it was not because he had
come fresh from the reading of Scott that his first
poems were ballads. He had an interest in the working
of men's minds as great as that of Browning, but,
being endowed with an artist's brain instead of that
of a logician, he had no desire to dissect or analyse,

---

[1] " Life and Letters," pp. 297, 414.
[2] *Ibid.*, p. 378.
[3] " Cornish Ballads," p. 286 note.
[4] There is evidence in " Tendrils " of the influence of all these except
Milton, and Hawker must early have known him, as his grandfather, the
Rev. R. Hawker, edited " Paradise Lost." (Memoir of R. Hawker, J. Williams, vol. I., p. 66).
[5] " Life and Letters," p. 311.

but was content simply to present the picture. For that the ballad was the only form. It was because he captured the spirit of the early ballads, which at their best portrayed as directly as possible some primitive passion, that his " Song of the Western Men " was taken to be genuinely old, for his theme is the courage of men and their devotion to a worthy leader. So in " Records of the Western Shore," though he has to take the legends as he finds them, and the theme of most is love, he gives also a picture of fear in " Mawgan of Melhuach," and of evil pride and simple faith in " The Bells of Bottreaux."

But for the second series of " Records " in 1836 he writes no ballads, for with his institution as Vicar of Morwenstow in 1834, the duties of the present become more urgent, and he finds problems connected with existence in his own age pressing themselves upon him. The poem on " Trebarrow " marks the transition, for of this Cornish spot he records,

> No legend cometh from beneath
> Of chief with good sword at his side
> Or Druid in his tomb of pride.

Instead there is a lesson to be learnt from the things of nature.

> One quiet bird that comes to make
> Her lone nest in the scanty brake ;
> A nameless flower, a silent fern—

and they teach the course of life on earth—its continuity in the type, its cessation in the individual.

> Hark ! on the cold wings of the blast
> The future answereth to the past ;
> The bird, the flower may gather still,
> Thy voice shall cease upon the hill ! [1]

Hawker, however, was too deeply religious by nature to be satisfied with such a gospel of despair, and in every other poem where he considers the wonders of creation, they point him to Nature's God. In " Pater

[1] Cornish Ballads." p, 39.

Vester Pascit Illa " and " The Sea-bird's Cry " he recognises that even the life of a sea-bird may teach the lesson of the protecting care of God for all He has created.

> Thou didst provide, e'en for this nameless bird
> Home, and a natural love, amid the surging seas.[1]

But while Nature may lead man to God, its teaching must be completed by that of the Christian faith, and in " Minster Church " Hawker sums up his position.

> Wake ! Dreamer of the Past ; no fairer grace
> Dwelt in the vale or glided o'er the plain.
> Heaven's changeless smile is here—earth's constant face ;
> The mingling sighs of woodland and the main.
> Here at lone eve, still seek this simple fane
> Hearts that would cherish, 'midst their native trees,
> A deathless faith—a hope that is not vain ;
> The tones that gather'd on the ancient breeze ;
> The Minster's pausing psalm ; the chorus of the seas.[2]

Unfortunately for Hawker he lived at a time when men were not taking the doctrines of the Christian faith for granted, and while his mystical intuition kept his vision clear in spite of the obstacles raised by materialism and scepticism, his reverence for tradition made him load himself with the various interpretations which men of different ages have given to those doctrines. He could no longer keep his eyes fixed on the goal, for he had to inspect his burden, and his progress was brought to a stop while he debated how much of it he should continue to carry. He writes in 1862 of " having for so many years wasted irrevocable time in resolution of doubt,"[3] and though the conflict grew more acute as he grew older, it was probably present even as early as this. He writes in 1862 of a book— " Hey's Lectures on the Articles," of which he had made a summary in 1831—2, " It was a Granary of ' Essays and Reviews.' I read and I doubted the total Revelation. My Notes contain at this day each an

---

[1] " Cornish Ballads, p. 40.
[2] *Ibid.*, p. 44.
[3] " Life and Letters," p. 388.

embryon of a modern infidelity. The Book was a Seed-plot of Schism and Disbelief." The rest of the letter gives the key to his theological position. " A Friend referred me to the Summa of St. Thomas Aquinas. I read and I was rescued. I found therein every question in Theology that can enter into the imagination of a Man discussed pro and con with the reference laid down and the authorities. Since then I have made it my solitary Book."[1] So from 1835, when he first began to study Aquinas, Hawker tends to exalt his reasoning powers above those of his imagination, and the song of the poet is at last drowned by the arguments of the theologian.[2]

A foreshadowing of this can be seen in the notes of 1838 quoted in the " Life and Letters." His medita-tions on the Psalms and his view of Ordination pro-claim the poet, but very ominous for the future are the thoughts on the Eucharist. " The Catholic Church de-fines the Eucharist to be a communication of the Great Sacrifice. The Romanists say a Perpetuation. Now *cf.* . . . We say *a* change, though not *the* Romanist change. We assert *a* Presence, though not *the* incar-nate Presence."[3] Very significant is the note to " Ephphatha " in " Ecclesia," 1840. " I have sought in these verses, to suggest a shadow of that beautiful instruction to Christian men, the actual and spiritual presence of our Lord in the second Sacrament of his Church ; a primal and perpetual doctrine in the faith once delivered to the Saints. How sadly the simplicity of this hath and has been distorted and disturbed by the gross and sensuous notion of a carnal presence in-troduced by the Romish innovators of the eleventh century," especially when we find it shortened in 1846 to the following. " I have sought in these verses to

[1] " Life and Letters," p. 385.
[2] The fourth verse of " The Wail of the Cornish Mother," which refers to Baptism, was added after 1840. It breaks the sequence of the thought which had before dealt solely with the mother's grief, and shows Hawker the artist giving way to Hawker the dogmatist.
[3] " Life and Letters," pp. 126, 127.

suggest the manner of that miraculous event, the actual and etherial Presence of Our Lord in the Second Sacrament of His Church." And after 1846 Hawker's poetical expression was limited to scattered pieces, while his thoughts " went down in MS.," and a glance at these shows how full his mind was of theological questions.

He was not from the beginning hostile to Rome, for in spite of much false doctrine she holds the Catholic Faith, but he was concerned with repudiating any claim of hers to jurisdiction over England. In 1846 he declares " England's Independence proclaimed in Two Statutes before the Reformation," and " The Old Priests, Queen Mary's Priests, were English and not Italian ; Catholic not Roman."[1] In 1849 he adds, " The Patriarch of the Greek Church doth not claim any jurisdiction in England. Why the Italian ? "[2] It is his zeal in upholding the Catholic Faith that makes him so bitter against Dissent, for in the Evangelicalism of his time he saw only a worship which consisted of " getting rid of God as much as possible in Church and yet keeping up appearances,"[3] and so degraded was the form of Methodism which was rife in Cornwall that he could describe its chief doctrine as being " sensual perception of the Holy Ghost."[4] Insistence on Catholic doctrine by a man of Hawker's character was bound to lead him very close to Roman thought, for, by dwelling on the value of tradition, and denying a man's right to think for himself in theology, in his religious life he tended to follow the course of that branch of the Catholic Church which laid more stress on the letter than on the spirit, and so gave an opening to superstition. His choice of St. Thomas Aquinas rather than one of the early Fathers for study would lead him the same way, for by the twelfth century many of the definitely Roman doctrines had appeared, and his

[1] " Stones Broken from the Rocks," p. 94.
[2] *Ibid.*, p. 95.
[3] *Ibid.*, p. 100.
[4] *Ibid.*, p. 102.

own love of outward beauty in worship, as symbolic of spiritual things, made him employ forms and ceremonies akin to those of Rome. This places him apart from the little body of seventeenth century mystics with which in other ways he has so much in common, for Herbert's poetry was inspired by his realisation of God's call to his own soul and its response, and Traherne had so pure a vision that he saw only the deceits of Rome, while Henry More, being more of a philosopher and less of a poet than Hawker, was able to avoid the dangers, though he saw the necessity of declaring before his death his belief in the doctrines taught by the Anglican Church.

What really led Hawker astray into the blind alley of controversial theology was a desire for knowledge for its own sake—an attitude against which he had been warned in the spiritual experience described in the letter to Mr. West quoted in an earlier chapter. Yet though there are notes on the Eucharist like the following—" A Mystery ! Thank God it is. God is all mystery. If from Him it needs must be a mystery. No Mystery—No God," and " The Real Presence is there but in most ineffable manner. Language cannot express how. Words cannot delineate nor tongue utter although the mind can conceive,"[1] there are other passages which show him striving to put into words what the Sacrament means to him. The result with its echo of the language of St. Thomas sounds very much like a belief in Transubstantiation. " Not a change of form or aspect or taste, but of substance. Not an alteration of shape or hue or sense, but of the Thing. Res habens quidditatem. A Law quenching Law. A Law of vast and boundless change, disdaining the accidents. The transit of one substance into another with disdain of the senses, with contempt of the accidents—so supernatural—the natural features remain as forgotten things."[2] This attitude towards the super-

[1] " Stones Broken from the Rocks," p. 121.
[2] Ibid., p. 124.

G

natural is not that of the mystic, but of the believer in magic, and, as we have seen, all Hawker's sense of the spiritual was liable to be degraded. The same tendency appears again in his later views of the Sacrament of Baptism in his belief in the efficacy of exorcism.

It is a thankless task to pursue Hawker's thought into questions which have been for centuries the causes of controversy and division in the Church of Christ. It shows him affected in a very real way by the age in which he lived, and his work sinks in value just so far as it is tainted by nineteenth century theological arguments. Through this both parties in the Catholic Church look at him askance, and men outside the Church ignore him, whereas if he had kept the vision clear, he would have had a message for men of every grade of opinion within and without the Church, for his own and for succeeding generations. For he started with a vision of the beauty and truth of the Catholic Faith, of its power of directing and satisfying the intellectual, moral and spiritual natures of men, and of its ever-abiding mystery. And a declaration of that was just what the men of the Victorian age needed. They had the Tractarians and learnt from them the beauty of Catholic doctrine, but had but confused ideas of its truth ; they had Tennyson and Browning, and learnt from them many lessons on intellectual, moral and spiritual subjects, but no one showed them the intimate connection between the faith, to which they strove so earnestly to cling, and life. That was the work which only a poet and a mystic churchman could do, and only in so far as Hawker did it was he of use to the men of his time, and only in this has he a message for " future men."

The volume, " Ecclesia," of 1840 shows him making the attempt. He tells in simple words the story of the Incarnation in a poem on " The Lady's Well ; " the theme of " The Signals of Levi " is the birth of Christ. " Morwennae Statio " points out the lessons which

may be learnt from the building which is the material
witness to the spiritual Church which He founded, and
" The Font," " Confirmation " and " Ephphatha "
deal with aspects of His worship. In " ' I am the
Resurrection and the Life ! ' saith the Lord," and
" The Butterfly," Hawker shows that nature holds the
lesson of the soul's resurrection, which is one of the
fundamentals of Christianity, and in so doing links
himself with all those mystics, Vaughan included, who
have pointed out the symbolic value of the life-history
of a butterfly. But though " Reeds Shaken with the
Wind " of 1843 and 1844 contain a few poems of this
type, though in the concluding couplet of " Marham
Church and Morwenstow," Hawker says,

> Let not the Dreamer-of-the-Past complain—
> The Saints, the Sanctuaries, the Creed, this very day remain ! "[1]

they do not form the main inspiration of the volume,
and we have to wait for nearly twenty years for the
poems which are the logical successors of the 1840
ones. " Aishah Schechinah," " that poem wherein I
am said to have rehearsed the Incarnation in a way
not yet found in the language,"[2] as Hawker describes
it, appeared in 1859, and in 1863, " The Quest of the
Sangraal " with its account of the incidents in Christ's
life on earth. And during those twenty years Hawker
had amassed much other material, not by any means
of universal acceptance, which became part of his
belief.

There are some who have seen Hawker as the plaything of circumstance—a man of great powers moulded into an eccentric by a life of seclusion passed in
close contact with wild nature, and though when we
study his life we see that he was indeed master of his
fate, and deliberately chose his path, we must guard
against the opposite danger of ignoring the influence
of his surroundings. That he was profoundly affected

[1] " Cornish Ballads," " The Saintly Names," p. 50.
[2] " Life and Letters," p. 443.

by the special beauty of Cornish scenery and by his peculiar isolation all will be ready to admit, but all the evidence is against the suggestion that his life would have been very different if he had been Vicar of some busy town parish. The beauty of nature would still have appealed to him, he would still have flung himself heart and soul into his duties, and he might easily have had no more communion with other minds than he had at Morwenstow, for even as a boy he loved solitude. What would have been missing, however, is the unique direction given to his love of the mediæval, and for that Morwenstow and its inhabitants must be held chiefly responsible.

Hawker's interest in the mediæval had nothing of the Victorian attitude in it. Starting, as were most of the men of his day directly or indirectly, indebted to Scott for awakening his enthusiasm, his path very soon left theirs, and he ended in a position far removed from those of Browning, or Ruskin, or the Pre-Raphaelites. They, with all their sympathy with its spirit, were able to stand away from it, for they had to create its atmosphere in their own imaginations ; Hawker lived in its midst. The superstitions and traditions which he heard from the lips of his parishioners were a heritage of the days when men consulted astrologers and burned witches ; the rites of the country-side at harvest, " a vestige of better and more pious times, when in all things God was acknowledged and praised," and the church itself a witness in stone to the faith of those

> who reared, with stern and trusting hands
> These dark grey towers of days unknown.[2]

The passage of two centuries had barely touched the beliefs of country folk, and Hawker found in Morwenstow the same spirit that Herrick found in Bemerton. The interesting resemblance between the two poets is due almost entirely to the similarity of their position.

[1] " Life and Letters," p. 113.
[2] " Cornish Ballads," p. 47.

Certainly they must have had a slight mental affinity
in that both found the pig a suitable domestic pet, but
life for one was a feast, for the other a fight. Only the
fact that both found charms and country festivals
flourishing in their parishes has brought about the
likeness.

But while Herrick gained little inspiration from the
forms of the Church, Hawker's love of them led him
still further into the spirit of the past. The symbolism
of Gothic architecture was a will-o'-the-wisp to a man
of his type, for it gave him a glimpse of the workings
of the mediæval mind, and led him to investigate
further. Had he been satisfied with the two types of
the Middle Ages with which he was familiar—Dante
and St. Thomas Aquinas—he could not have gone
very far wrong, but he chose a third teacher, and the
blame for much of Hawker's later extravagance in
thought must be laid at the door of a Victorian—and
an Oxford man, who introduced him to the study of
Gretser. In 1849 Hawker advised " the slanderers of
God's servants . . . to read carefully and thoroughly
the works of Gretser, published in Latin, in 17 folio
volumes, at Ratisbon 1734—41," and there can be no
doubt that J. B. Morris, " Union Jack " Morris, made
it possible for him to read Gretser, for he lent him a
volume which was still in his possession in 1860.[1]
Hawker spent three years in translating and analys-
ing the work of this writer, and the mediæval love of
symbolism and allegory—so often far-fetched and
strained—sank into his mind, and coloured all his later
thought.

It is the old story of Fancy usurping the throne of
Imagination. Hawker the mystic could write, " The
flowers put on their robes with loveliness each after
their kind and are happy in the sun. They drink the
dews of even and bend their brows in thanksgiving.
To-morrow they fade and die—die happy. They have
served God's purpose with their beautiful array and

[1] " Life and Letters," pp. 375, 376.

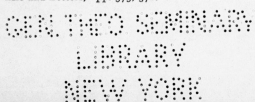

adorned the world of God. God's care for the little proves his care for the great."[1] Hawker in the grip of the mediæval wrote, " The rose and the lily were created to be emblems of our Blessed Lord and His Mother,"[2] and "Columbine, a flower emblematic of the Holy Ghost and named from the Dove,"[3] and " Shamrock. A Spanish type of the Trinity brought by them into Ireland."[4] Hawker the mystic wrote, " Compare ' Prometheus Bound,' the climax of Pagan conception of the Sublime, with the Cross. It is not profane so to do, because it shows how far more deeply He on the wood knew what was in Man. Cf. ' I can revenge '— with ' Father, forgive.' Which phrase causes most the breast to bound and the eyes to fill ? "[5] But he also spent valuable time over the symbolic meaning of the outward events of the Crucifixion and the Burial. " The Quest of the Sangraal " is full of his conclusions.

> Pilate the Roman—doomster for all lands
> Or else the Judgment had not been for all—
> Bound Jesu-Master to the world's tall tree,[6]

a thought borrowed from Dante, is completed in the MS. notes by the thought, " He died *whole* to symbolize an unsevered church. Not a bone broken."[7]

" Westward Lord Jesu looked His latest love,"[8] with its explanatory note, is another, and packed with symbolic meaning are the lines,

> So, too, Lord Jesu from His mighty tomb
> Cast the dear shadow of His red right hand
> To soothe the happy South—the angel's home.[9]

We have only to turn to letters quoted in the " Life "[10] to show how much thought went to the composition of

1 " Stones Broken from the Rocks," p. 62.
2 *Ibid.*, p. 63.
3 " Life and Letters," p. 104.
4 " Stones Broken from the Rocks," p. 64.
5 *Ibid.*, p. 8.
6 " Cornish Ballads," p. 174.
7 " Stones Broken from the Rocks," p. 8.
8 " Cornish Ballads," p. 179.
9 *Ibid.*, p. 180.
10 *V.* " Life and Letters," pp. 428, 429, 451, 452.

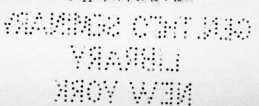

the one line,

> The bird of judgment chants the doom of night.[1]

Yet though " The Quest of the Sangraal " shows the pitfalls which lay before Hawker in his pursuit of the mediæval, it is itself the justification of his search. Touched at various points by other nineteenth century poems, which appear to be like it, it is yet unique. Without distorting the mediæval story as Tennyson did, Hawker has written a poem breathing the mediæval atmosphere as surely as any poem of Rossetti or William Morris, and yet, by the mediæval device of allegory, essentially modern in that it deals with Victorian problems. Mr. West writes of him as " one born some 500 years too late—a thoroughly mediæval and Dantesque mind,"[1] but the description is incomplete. Certainly with Dante and Aquinas as his intellectual leaders, he could hardly help arriving at the mediæval view of the Catholic Faith, but the Middle Ages would probably have burnt as a heretic for his independence of thought the man whom the nineteenth century accused of Roman Catholicism. Even his reverence for tradition could not stifle his own spiritual intuition, and in many ways his thought was ahead of even the nineteenth century position.

As a mystic Hawker had no doubts. However troubled he might be by theology, his insistence on the reality of spiritual things never faltered, and he spent his life in exploring the avenues of thought which led from that central fact. He was first and foremost a devotional mystic—one to whom spiritual insight came through the agency of revealed religion ; but the vision of God in nature followed hard upon the realisation of God through prayer and worship. The only mystical experience recorded in his poetry[2] showed this, and showed too his intuitive realisation of God's omnipresence, " the surrounding God," an

---

[1] " Cornish Ballads," p. 183.
[2] " Life and Letters," p. 644.
[3] *V.* " A Rapture on the Cornish Hills."

aspect of God on which in later years he loved to dwell. As God may be sought in Transcendence or Immanence, the mystic has to hold the balance in his mind. Hawker the poet and artist naturally tends to apprehend the Immanent God, but he sees the danger to which this theory lies open, and in his notes we see him trying to define his view, lest he should be drawn into the error of Pantheism, for he writes : " God, A Spirit. We must not say all things are full of God. This would make Him the material Spirit of the Universe, as pagan poets sang. But we must say, God contains all things. He holds the Orbs within His vast embrace. Our Globe is in the midst of God. The Sun travels on his courses, and the Godhead is around His way. You may measure with myriads of Miles the distances of the planets and the Stars, but your Mind is not able to conceive the Borders of the Circumfluent God."[1] His own consciousness of the spiritual was so intensely real that he was not content until he had tried to give a definition to " Spirit," even though he could express his idea only by negatives. " A pure thing of life. Nothing material or made. Mere unmingled existence. Nothing so gross as air. Conscious thrilling, alive. Without the labour of breath, without the effort of wings, uncontrolled by space, unapproached by time, unfettered by form."[2] Though the ordinary man is shut off from the realm of spirit by the things of sense, the mystic living in this material world is an exile from his native land, for, says Hawker, as did Swedenborg and Blake before him, " to be happy we must go out of ourselves, but not into the carnal world. We must close our eyes, as it were, to our own fleshly existence and realise the spiritual things that are round about and very nigh to every one of us. The angelic myriads ascending in a graduated rank from the surrounding earth to God ; the diffused of God. The contact of the Holy Ghost."[3] But he found no

[1] " Stones Broken from the Rocks," p. 3.
[2] *Ibid.*, p. 23.
[3] *Ibid.*, p. 24.

word to express the intimate connection which he perceived between every thing spiritual, and so coined the word " Numyne." The development of this idea we must trace in detail, for though its history dates back to man's earliest dealings with the supernatural, Hawker's treatment of it was entirely original, and his conclusions are both inspiring and suggestive, for he seems to have laid hold on a secret towards which modern speculation is still groping.

In 1859 Hawker records, " Ten, fifteen years agone I received knowledge of this element (i.e., the Atmosphere of God and Angels) and called it Numyne."[1] Though he evidently took his conclusions to be Divinely inspired, the suggestion seems to have come from meditation on a form of words, judging from the following note. " Knum, the old Sethic word for the God of the Water—thence all Divinity was entitled Numen —thence came Nomen : thus Nomen and Numen were interchanged. Cf. ' Go Baptize in Nomine P. F. and S. S.' or in Numine. Therefore whatsoever of the Divine Essence exists anywhere or in any Person or Thing I (R. S. H.) name

NUMYNE.

Cf. also an original interchange of Lumen and Numen."[2] From that beginning the next step was given by nature, for " if all material things are but sacraments of God,"[3] the atmosphere, to which physical experiments were then turning popular attention, must have lessons for mankind of as much value as those given by " every tree, animal and rock." The properties of the electric wave, unseen but exerting tremendous power, are surely symbolic of Divine grace, man's use of that wave in telegraphy a reminder of the communion of saints. Hawker becomes lyrical and almost prophetic on this. " In these days when thought leaps to thought and lives along the

[1] " Stones Broken from the Rocks," p. 25.
[2] " Life and Letters," p. 255.
[3] " Stones Broken from the Rocks," p. 44.

wire—when soul answereth to soul with leagues and leagues between—when, at signal given, hearts beat with sudden sympathy with hearts beyond the Seas— when the wish of a Man shall thrill from land to land suddenly—when by and by a voice will girdle the whole earth with a King's supreme command in the twinkling of an eye, amid scenery such as this we may easily conceive the transit of Prayer from Saint to Saint and the swift rush of desire from Angel to Angel, and the gliding chariots of the Air with grace and blessing full."[1]

Man's experiments in psychology add a new idea, probably Hawker's own, though he might have found it in Swedenborg. " Mesmerism uncloses a vast field of thought as to the mode of spiritual influence upon us. If a Man by his look or gaze and the impress of his hands can urge his power into our very will, what may not angels and spirits who have access to such fine thin airy channels of communication do with us ? "[2] Here his religion gives right direction to the new thought, and prevents him from indulging in psychic experiments for their own sake. " The truth is that what they call magnetism is the casualty which has jarred the wires of the Holy Catholic Church. Call it Spiritual Magnetism. Understand it of the intercourse of Saints. Use it for communion by texture of the Church, and all is manifest, all holy, all true."[3] " Numyne " can now be described as " a sea etherial with tides of air. Its throne and orb amidst the Orient. There and thence it loosens and it binds the stars. *It is* that unseen Magnet of the One which is mated and linked and blended with the Sun."[4] And, following the other train of thought, as " the atmosphere of mind."[5] It only needed a reference to the luminiferous ether in one of Hawker's favourite books, Sir D.

---

[1] " Stones Broken from the Rocks," p. 27.
[2] *Ibid.*, p. 38.
[3] *Ibid.*, p. 39.
[4] *Ibid.*, p. 26.
[5] *Ibid.*, p. 25.

Brewster's " More Worlds than One," to add the
coping-stone to his " castle in the air," and to give us
the note in which are woven together all the different
strands of thought. " Now what shall link and blend
the existence of God the Trinity with the Things of
Space and Time ? A Sacramental Sea of Light—An
atmosphere alive with Schechinah—An Essence that,
like a Sacrament, should blend Mind and Matter, God
and Man—A Substance (Res habens quidditatem)
that can inherit the mutual attributes of the Spiritual
and Material World—An Element so rarified, so thin,
elastic, pure, that it forms the Medium or Woof wherein the Solar Light undulates, glances and glides ; so
holy and divine, that it is the native Atmosphere of
Angels and Spiritual Things, and so replete with Godhead that therewithal The Celestial Persons can become tangible to the Senses, insomuch that clothed in
that Numyne a Man can perceive and adore the Glory
of God."[1]

It is quite clear that Hawker thought he had been
vouchsafed knowledge of a " new Element," and imagined his description of it original. Yet he was only
" spreading the news which a long line of practical
mystics had been crying for centuries into the deaf
ears of mankind."[2] In the space of two centuries before him the same thought had been repeated again
and again. In " Religio Medici," Sir Thomas Browne
had written, " Do but extract from the corpulency of
bodies, or resolve things beyond their First Matter,
and you discover the habitation of Angels : which if
I call it the ubiquitary and omnipresent Essence of
God, I hope I shall not offend Divinity."[3] In his " High
and Deep Searching-out of the Three-fold Life of Man,"
Jacob Boehme had tried to express in sublime ab-
stractions his vision of " the virgin of the wisdom of
God," by which he meant " the whole deep of the

[1] " Life and Letters," p. 255.
[2] E. Underhill. " Mysticism," p. 316, referring to Wm. Law.
[3] " Everyman " Edition, p. 39.

Deity without end or number."[1] He had described
" this wisdom of God " as " the substantiality of the
spirit which the spirit of God putteth on as a garment
whereby He manifesteth Himself,"[2] and " that substantiality " as " the element of God, for there is a life
therein (but without understanding) in which the
paradise of God consisteth."[3] William Law had handed
on Boehme's message for English readers. " In Eternal Nature, or the Kingdom of Heaven, materiality
stands in life and light ; it is the light's glorious Body,
or that garment wherewith light is clothed, and therefore has all the properties of life in it, and only differs
from light as it is its brightness and beauty, as the
holder and displayer of all its colours, powers and
virtues."[4]

Some of Hawker's tentative developments of his
idea bring him even closer to the earlier mystics. We
must look in the notes to find all that was in his mind
when he gave the title " Aishah Schechinah " to the
Virgin Mary. We find first a question. " B.V.M. *cf.*
Might not God conceive and embody whatsoever was
Feminine in the Triune Essence, and so evolve *ante
secula* the Schechinah of Eve ? "[5] and later the fuller
note. " That image and impress effulgent, be it what it
may, when it had inhabited with life that imperial
mind of God, wherein to conceive is to create, that
image I say, be it a superangelic soul or be it an eman-
ation of all that was Woman or feminine in the Divine
Essence could pass away no more. It stood before the
thought of God royally : the eternal Spouse ; the
Schechinah of God's own Bride : the Virgin Mother of
Divinity ; the etherial essence of the future Mother of
God."[6] Hawker's mind is working in the same way as
Boehme's and Blake's. Boehme writes, " In the eternal

[1] " Three-fold Life of Man," p. 56.
[2] *Ibid.*, p. 135.
[3] *Ibid.*, p. 53.
[4] " An Appeal to All who Doubt," Liberal and Mystical Writings of Wm. Law, p. 52.
[5] " Stones Broken from the Rocks," p. 13.
[6] *Ibid.*, p. 14.

virgin, God became man."[1] Blake among all the various
symbols under which he describes this " fourth principle " has that of " the Covering Cherub," and in " The
Everlasting Gospel " identifies it with the Virgin.
Hawker touches on the idea of the mirror of God,
which we find in both Boehme and Blake, when he
writes, " Saints see us all as in a glass, we gleam before them in the vision of God . . . We inhabit God the
Sea. But our Ocean is alive and can breathe in silent
Power from Saint to Saint Communion of the Deep."[2]
Though his language is much more material, Hawker's
thought on the Sacraments is akin to that of Boehme.

It appears, then, that Hawker's idea is not as original as he imagined it. Some may even think that his
brain is presenting to him as new thought material
which he acquired in his wide reading at Oxford, and
which had lain sub-consciously in his mind, but there
is no evidence that he had ever read Boehme or Blake.[3]
The mystical attitude of mind, combined with meditation on similar material, is quite enough to account
for the likeness, and there can be no doubt that most
of Hawker's theory is based on ideas presented by the
Bible and the early Fathers. His conclusions are therefore all the more interesting, in that by a road of his
own making he arrives at the same goal as many before him have done.

Still more important is his way of approach—meditation on scientific discoveries. Hawker was the only
nineteenth century mystic to see the unity underlying
all the new ideas, the solid ground beneath what seemed to the Victorians shifting sand. Tennyson could
offer no help in that way, for his feet were set no firmer
than theirs, and Browning did not understand their
difficulties, for he had found a path on the solid rock.
Only Hawker saw that discoveries in physics and
psychology were pointing towards the truth that only

[1] " Three-fold Life of Man," p. 188.
[2] " Stones Broken from the Rocks," p. 27.
[3] He may have known of Boehme through Coleridge.

the spiritual is the real, and therefore his thought is
still peculiarly applicable to this age marked by
further discoveries in the composition of the material
world. It has been pointed out[1] that Swedenborg in his
scientific descriptions of the First Element or " aura "
seems to have anticipated modern thought on the subject of the ether ; may we not claim that Hawker also
had knowledge of this element, and that his idea
seems not only in accord with the most recent discoveries, but even stretches beyond them ? Many
modern physicists are content to ignore the ether, for
it " may not be thought of . . . as consisting of parts
which may be tracked through time."[2] It is only something which " helps to determine mechanical (and
electro-magnetic) events."[3] Hawker's " Numyne,"
" neither Life nor Matter—neither Vital or inert, but
both—between both—life-giving rather than alive,"[4]
is an element in which light, electricity and magnetic
forces travel, but it is something more—it is the medium for thought. As the study of physics becomes apparently more immaterial, and that of psychology
apparently more material, may we not also arrive at
Hawker's standpoint ?[5] Moreover, his idea seems to be
connected with that side of the philosophy of M.
Bergson, which deals with the theory of rhythm, for,
as scientists have discovered that it is only necessary
to alter the rate of vibration for the sensation of light
to become that of sound, who shall dare to say that
there is not an infinite series of vibrations, of most of
which only spirits are conscious ?

The men of Hawker's own time had no chance of
passing judgment on his theory of " Numyne," for the
article on that subject which he sent to " Willis's Cur-

---

[1] " Principia," ed. Rendell and Tansley, 1912.   Introd. pp. xlv.–xlvii.
[2] Einstein, " Ether and Relativity," p. 23.
[3] Ibid., p. 19.
[4] Unpublished MS.
[5] Sir Oliver Lodge has already reached it.   V. " Ether and Reality,"
1925, p. 179.   The Ether . . . " is the primary instrument of Mind, the
vehicle of Soul, the habitation of Spirit.   Truly it may be called the living
garment of God."

rent Notes " was returned " well-thumbed by some
one," but was never printed. It would probably receive the same treatment to-day, yet in his theory
Hawker saw something which, though above and beyond the limits of Time and Space, yet bound all
creation, past, present, future, material and spiritual,
and which was, until his idea became degraded through
his insistence on the material, full of inspiration. It
linked the Scriptures with every-day life, for Genesis
I. 2 told of its creation. "The forefathers called it the
spiritual or ethereal element, ' caelum '."[1] Its existence
is recorded in many instances in the Old Testament by
the appearance of the Schechinah, " the cloudy signal
of the Presence," of which " Numyne " is " the sacramental element,"[2] for by it man received knowledge of
the presence of God through his senses. But while
" the Old Church subserved to revelation, the New
Church revealed." " The Old Church guarded the
Oracle, the New Church was the Oracle itself. All was
to be real in Christ. His Church was to be the Thing."[3]
Then " Numyne " has its function, for " the Holy
Catholic Church is a vast sphere of bankless and boundless element, filled with vibrations from Saint to
Saint, and from Saint to Angels and God."[4] " God,
the Spirit, is the Firmament, the expansive Essence,
the embracing and enfolding Element. Then the
Church is the woof, the texture. The Church enchains
in one, embodies, links, communes, conveys the Triune God, the Lord Jesu, We in Him and He in us.
Weaves into one Body from the top throughout Christ
by a network which we name Communion of Saints."[5]

How often has the Church forgotten that her sole
mission is to show Christ to the world, that, as in this
span of existence spirit cannot express itself without
body, by a symbol the Church is the means by which

[1] V. note to " Sangraal," " Cornish Ballads," p. 184.
[2] V. note to " Aishah Schechinah," " Cornish Ballads," p. 162.
[3] " Stones Broken from the Rocks," p. 83.
[4] Ibid.
[5] Ibid., p. 85.

Christ works in the world, and therefore her only work is "to breathe God's thoughts, to deliver God's tidings, to speak God's words, to do God's deeds."[1] Spiritual arrogance has too often blotted out the vision ; dogma taken the place of love. The tragedy is reflected in Hawker's own life, and in the Church of his time, which, with its hollow conservatism, its cowardice in the face of new thought, drove men like Matthew Arnold and Clough to scepticism. But Hawker's mysticism brought him back to his ideal, and made him, in spite of his backsliding, able to teach his contemporaries. We can see him in the letters becoming more tolerant, more humble, more inspired. The man who so hated Dissent in his youth learnt to write to Mrs. Watson in 1861 of her Baptist servant—" Never mind what sect. He or she can't be wrong whose life is in the right."[2] The man of strong will and high temper wrote in his notes on " Christ" : " ' Learn of me.' What ? To create an orb ? To enkindle a star ? Nay, but to be meek ! meek as a God ! lowly of heart like the Omnipotent ! gentle as the Judge of quick and dead !"[3] The man who placed so much value on tradition became one who welcomed new thought, and found in the Bible his guide for all.

However far afield Hawker's thought may stray, his conclusions never rest outside the confines of the Divine revelation in the Scriptures. He reads Swedenborg, and, though no doubt attracted by much of his writing, condemns him for " pretending to be real. If he had called his Works Speculative Theories, or even Fantasies, their injurious tendencies might have been subdued . . . No account of a State Future to us that is contradictory to Holy Writ is fit to enter a Christian mind."[4] His faith in the Bible never wavers at any attack of materialistic science against it. He writes in his notes, " Not only was God obliged to speak to men

1 " Stones Broken from the Rocks," p. 83.
2 " Life and Letters," p. 345.
3 " Stones Broken from the Rocks," p. 6.
4 " Life and Letters," p. 350.

in the language of men, but to employ that state of language which was contemporary with the Era of Revelation. To the Jews of Joshua, for example, a rude and elementary mode of expression was natural." " If the language of God had anticipated in any science the discoveries of that science it would have been unintelligible until the discovery was made."[1] So the geologist's discovery of the age of the earth, which was so devastating to the Victorian's inborn sense of his own importance in the scheme of creation, only offered Hawker the opportunity of insisting on the existence of "myriads, myriads of intellectual creatures," which " descended, and descend, in gradual attribute from God the bodiless to Adam the First Man. Which Race or Kind of these, may have peopled or dwelt in the awful Scenery of the Pre-Adamite Earth, we do not yet know. But there was something strongly congenial with the Majestic Nature of the Seraph and the Archangel in the vast and ponderous adjuncts of that wondrous World."[2]

Darwin's discovery of the process of evolution was only another opening for Hawker's mystical thought. After summing up " the achievements of fixed and natural laws among the atomic materials," declared by the scientists to be " under the vibration of the forces alone," he asks, " whence did these atoms derive their existence ; and from what and from whom do they inherit the propensities wherewithal they are imbued ? And tell me, most potent seignors, what is the origin of these forces ? And with whom resides the impulse of their action and the guidance of their control ? ' Nothing is so difficult as a beginning.' Your philosopher is mute ! he has reached the horizon of his domains, and to him all beyond is doubt, and uncertainty and guess. We must lift the veil . . . We perceive the realms of surrounding space peopled by immortal creatures of the air—

[1] " Stones Broken from the Rocks," p. 71.
[2] *Ibid.*, p. 72.

H

> Myriads of spiritual things that walk unseen
> Both when we wake and when we sleep.

These are the existences, in aspect as " young men in white garments," who inhabit the void place between the worlds and their Maker, and their God . . . These are they that each with a delegated office fulfil that their ' King Invisible ' decrees ; not with the dull, inert mechanism of fixed and Natural Law, but with the unslumbering energy and the rational obedience of spiritual Life. They mould the atom ; they wield the force ; and, as Newton rightly guessed, they rule the World of matter beneath the silent Omnipotence of God."[1] His own imagination working on the logical reasoning of St. Thomas Aquinas took a short cut to the conclusions reached by later thinkers. " When the Stony doubt hardened as to the conflict between geologic and mosaic Time I sought the Oracle. Said He in the Words of St. Augustine, The Days of Moses cannot be Solar Days, because until the 4th the Sun was not created. What then were they ? Seven Scenic Sections of Revelation to the Angels for delivery to Man. This with his clear and stern definition of Time closes every question, settles every doubt—Time, the measure of movement having a former and a later point."[2] So he was ready with an answer when Colenso attacked "the chronology of Holy Writ." " My little children at the school would teach him that whereas in Heaven Time does not exist there could be no such thing regarded in inspiration as Dates or Periods or Years."[3]

Hawker's thoughts on Time and Space are full of interest. While mountains of doubt loomed large before his contemporaries, Hawker from his loftier position looked right over them. " What can we tell about dates after all ? Time is nothing but Adam's clock—a measurement that men invented to reckon by."[4] The

[1] " Western Morning News," September 9th, 1874.   Printed in " Life and Letters," p. 122.
[2] " Life and Letters," p. 386.
[3] *Ibid.*, p. 481.
[4] " Footprints," p. 105.

words are recorded as those of Daniel Gumb, but it is quite obvious that Hawker has invented them for him. The thought is completed in the notes. " Whereby do they reckon in Heaven ? Not by days and nights— they have none. Not by sun course of our system. They have no usage of our planets or signs. By no procession of equinoxes derived from us. How do they reckon there ? Then what folly to calculate, by our little millennial data, what the Lord of Eternity will do. The Moth ! The Moth ! "[1] We have here the reason why Hawker, in spite of his enquiring mind, was not led into attempts to decipher prophecies by mathematical calculation, as were some of those to whom he is most akin.

Hawker considers Space, too, as from a point outside it. We find the conclusion of his thoughts in a note in the " Sangraal." " Space is a created thing, material and defined. As time is *mensura motus*, so is space *mensura loci* ; and it signifies that part of God's presence which is measured out to enfold the planetary universe. The tracery of its outline is a cone. Every path of a planet is a curve of that conic figure ; and as motion is the life of matter, the whirl of space on its allotted courses is the cause of that visible movement of the sun and the solar system towards the star Alcyone as the fixed centre in the cone of space."[2] Did he know that his intellectual kinsman, Henry More, had been before him in giving to Space the figure of a cone ?[3] Probably not, for he evidently considers it an original idea, and, in his letter to Dean Cowie[4] explaining his use of it, the only suggestions seem to have come from Aquinas. And certainly in the development of the thought he was original, and ahead of his time, for in one of the paragraphs in the MS. notes he seems to anticipate Einstein. The extract runs as follows : " Creation gave existence and form, life and

[1] " Stones Broken from the Rocks," p. 48.
[2] " Cornish Ballads," p. 178.
[3] " Poems of Henry More," ed. Grosart, p. 160.
[4] " Life and Letters," p. 374.

fountains of force to such a star. Two powers at work, intellect and will. The Thoughts of God glided into existence and form underneath the force of His Will. *Cf.* that Force permanent still. Which was first breathed, Time or Space ? *Me judice*—Time, because in it all went forth. No Right Angles or Lines. All elliptic curves. The Arches of the Air."[1] Hawker certainly seems to be feeling for a geometry which will take into consideration something more than the three dimensions of Space. If there was existence in Time only, before Space was created, Time must play its part in all ideas on Space. And Hawker seems to make Time itself almost of no account when he brings the wisdom of Plato, invigorated by Christianity, to launch a bark which sails from him

> like a sinking star
> Beyond the utmost bound of human thought.

But Hawker's excursions into the realm of science are but tentative. He had not the intellect or training which enabled Swedenborg to be so far ahead of his time in scientific speculation. Moreover, Hawker's mind was not capable of a sustained flight in the rarefied atmosphere of pure thought, and the fetters of fantastic symbolism drag him back to earth. With naïve delight he fits his theory of the cone of space into " the doctrine of signatures," for " a cone is a pyramid in motion," and he sees in Space " the reflex imagery of God." It is " as though God the Trinity had imprinted on a region of the Universe His own Symbol the Pyramid, and then, by impulse of motion which is to Stars life, conveyed that centrifugal whirl which proceeds to this day."[2] The whole note reminds us forcibly of the thought of Jacob Boehme, but a little search shows at once both the point of contact, and the wide difference between them. Hawker writes, " *Cf.* the Wheel Alive," but the addition of the words, " of the Prophet's ken," show that he has in mind the

---

[1] " Stones Broken from the Rocks, "p. 43.
[2] *Ibid.*, p. 49.

vision of Ezekiel ; he refers to the laws of motion, but
derives no symbolic meaning from them. Yet the link
with Boehme is here, for Hawker has learnt of the
laws of motion from his study of Newton, and Newton
derived his theory from the philosophy of Boehme.
But Hawker's symbolism here expresses no great
truths. Boehme's working-out of the three-fold principle in life, is like a great cathedral ; compared with
his thought, Hawker's efforts are but those of a child
building a castle of bricks.

Indeed it is not unjust to him to see likenesses to
those of a child in many of his mental processes ; he
has at times the same inconsequence, the same delight
in achievement, the same absence of a sense of proportion. He passes in a moment from prophet to child. We
may see the process repeated in his thought on the
Virgin Mary. We have already seen him striving to
reach the heights where Boehme and Blake breathe so
easily ; the depths to which he might fall are shown in
a letter from a certain J. H. S. published in the
" Church Review " for September 11th, 1875. The
writer states that Hawker had shown him, twenty
years before, " a scheme with symbols of the Trinity
and the Incarnation, of eternity and time, which he
had drawn out. As there was no place in eternity or
time for the crescent, the symbol of Mary, it was necessary to find a place for it in the Trinity and the Incarnation, and the admission of the Immaculate Conception followed as a matter of course." Hawker has
the delight of a child in making things fit into one
another. Perhaps it was this unconscious affinity with
children that made him consider them his equals in
mental stature, and give them a diagram to illustrate
his theories of Space and Time, which was founded on
the favourite symbol of the occultists, a triangle en-
closing the Hebrew word for " Jehovah " and itself
surrounded by a circle.[1] Certainly the pupils in his
school must have had an original education, for one of

[1] V. Lee, " Memorials," pp. 90, 91.

Miss Kuczynski's first letters reports that " he instils into the youthful mind of Morwenstow the most absurd superstitions about Ghosts and Brownies, which he believes actually exist."[1] We see here the warped development of another branch of inspiring thought.

Hawker's first description of angels was inspired by the desire to emphasize their spiritual reality. In his criticism of Dr. Lee's Newdigate Prize Poem in 1854 he writes, " Angels have no wings : not a single feather. Whensoever in the Old Testament or the New Testament they actually appear, they are expressly said to be ' young men in white garments ' not to be distinguished by the patriarchs from other youthful guests, and so entertained at unawares . . . Wings, moreover, are to me destructive of all poetry of motion from place to place. They imply effort. The angels glide on the chariots and horses of their own desires. One in Syria is fain to be in Egypt and immediately is there ; just as we think in one scene of a distant spot, and at once our minds behold it without consciousness of the space between . . . True, the prophetic imagery is abundant in feathers—symbolic every one. But the actual angels are real existing people, who walk and live and move in calm unalterable youth ; who speak in their unearthly language, although their voices do not move the air ; who pass among us, and the grass bends not where they tread." If he had gone no further than this, there would have been only beauty in his ideas of spiritual beings, but because his imagination was so much stronger than his reason, evil for him was personified by " more devils than vast hell can hold." It is one thing to see with mystic vision the extent of evil in the world, but the Christian mystic sees too that " there is a soul of goodness in things evil," and the man who thinks those who oppose him possessed by demons, and himself so especially the servant of God that demons raise storms to attack his material prosperity, has bartered his birthright for a mess of

[1] " Life and Letters," p. 444.

pottage, and his road is no longer an upward climb through open country, but a descent into the wood of Error with furtive glances behind him lest any of the dimly-seen figures should attack him unawares.

Yet even then the mystic might triumph. Writing of the destruction of his barn by a hurricane in March, 1866, he first ascribes it to the anger of " the Enemy of Man," but continues, " Nor is such an accident as mine a sign of God's displeasure. Whom he loves best he tries most and I have always regarded my trials in life as the touch of a Father's hand on the shoulder of His Child to keep him in the straight and narrow way that leadeth unto life."[1] We must guard against the danger of condemning all Hawker's references to demons as childish and superstitious. He was no philosopher and had little power of considering evil as an abstract thing ; we may almost hear Hawker speaking through the medium of Daniel Gumb's note-books. " Why should such harm be allowed to be done ? I read some reasons once in a book . . . called ' The Origin of Evil ' ; but I could not understand a word of it. My notion is that when evil somehow came into the world, God did not destroy it at once, because He is so almighty that He let it go on, to make manifest His power and majesty ; and so He rules over all things, and turns them into good at the last. N.B. The devil is called in the Bible the Prince of the Powers of the Air ; so he may be, but he must obey his Master. The poor wretch is but a slave after all ! " To Hawker · the forces of evil were spiritual activities of great power ; he therefore considered them as substantial beings, and, as always, his attempt to give his meaning sounds almost material. With an outlook closely akin to that of Blake on certain points, he draws very near to him in the exercise of his visual imagination. His vision may be often clouded, and his powers wavering, but he has the same love of describing unseen forces by presenting them in human form.

[1] " Life and Letters," pp. 538, 539.

Some of his most obscure pronouncements shine brightly when set free from their strange setting. Let us look, for instance, at some of his remarks on his own age. " One sign of the Demon never alters and that is cruelty. Cruelty is the distinctive feature of the nineteenth century. Consider Palmer — Dove — Bacon — Madeline Smith—Spollen, &c., and you find the principal point in their characters is selfish cruelty. A Tchutgar, say the Orientals, i.e., a Demon, never weeps—is pitiless."[1] Hawker the mystic is as alive as Blake was to the evil wrought in the world by selfishness and oppression. Or again, " The Weather is quite worthy of the Prince of the Powers of the Air to whom the atmosphere of this island is surrendered because of the great majority of Vassals of his own which exists in this Vulcanic nation. He won this pre-eminently by becoming the Baal of English worship and his ministering Demons have given up in return the Myths of Steam and Gas and the Oxydes for Anglican Reward."[2] Hawker saw that many of the discoveries in chemistry and physics led to destruction rather than progress, that experiments made with a view of ending war only resulted in making war more awful in its devastating consequences than ever before, and that the scientists of his time were men whose knowledge had made them materialistic, and it was then only logical for him to call their power " demoniac." As a mystic he knew that knowledge without love, knowledge pursued only for the sake of power, could never be anything but deadly in its effects. Turn to the transcript from his MS. book, entitled " £ s. d.", which he sent to Miss Twining in 1855, for his imaginative presentation of the fact that " The Sin of England has been Greed of Gold—Lust for Gain."[3] Hawker has overlaid the severity of " The love of money is the root of all evil," with strange trappings of his own design.

---

[1] " Life and Letters," p. 301.
[2] *Ibid.*, p. 547.
[3] *Ibid.*, p. 242.

Hawker's power of visual imagination shows itself in descriptions of other scenes in the world where " Time and the hour are not." His interest in human nature naturally led him to think of the lot of a spirit when it enters into Eternity, though he does not follow Aquinas and Dante in discussing psychology. He is concerned chiefly with the different standards of values in the material and spiritual worlds, and as he realised that "Great People are like little ones in their feelings, passions, love and hate,"[1] he seized on " great deaths," such as those of the Prince Consort and the Duke of Wellington, to conjure up the scene when the individual was " nothing but soul." Hawker blamed Swedenborg for his descriptions of Heaven and Hell, but he himself was almost material in his expression. Yet he was saved from indulging in unprofitable speculations on the manner of the life after death because he used his pictures to teach a lesson for the present—the vanity of earthly success. He saw distinctly all his life that the England of his time was gradually concentrating her energies on material progress rather than on spiritual, or even mental, growth, and all his comments on topical events show this attitude. No doubt some will see in them "a parochial character ... which will now-a-days provoke a smile,"[2] and Hawker does sometimes lose a sense of proportion, but, like Carlyle and Ruskin, he saw the men of his generation obsessed by the idea of material gain. " Mercantile Men," he writes, " amass large fortunes by demoniac help and call silver and gold prosperity."[3] His attitude towards riches was very close to Blake's. " To think that Earthly success, Earthly grandeur may be the direct gift of the Demon,"[4] writes Hawker, almost repeating the thought in Blake's lines :

> Since all the riches of this world
> May be gifts from the Devil and earthly kings,

[1] " Life and Letters," p. 302.
[2] *Ibid.*, p. 280.
[3] *Ibid.*, p. 535.
[4] *Ibid.*, p. 442.

> I should suspect that I worshipped the Devil
> If I thank'd my God for worldly things.[1]

Many of Hawker's utterances are those of a prophet crying " Woe ! " to a land which has forsaken God. They culminate, as do all his thoughts, in " The Quest of the Sangraal," the poem of which he wrote, " I fear there will be a want of relish for such a theme and that those who do like the Subject would rather I had discussed the money value of the Vase and its array of jewels and dealt with the Quest as a lucky speculation of Sir Galahad,"[2] and which draws to a close with the cry,

> Ah ! haughty England ! lady of the wave ! . . .
> What is thy glory in the world of stars ?

" The Quest of the Sangraal " is a unique poem. It is unfinished, and yet complete, old and yet new. It is an epic, yet few poems in English are more expressive of their authors, even though definitely lyrical in inspiration. It is obscure, and yet clear, for, though we cannot understand the poem without reading his other writings first, yet if we already know Hawker, it is with the joy of re-discovery that we see first one trait and then another hidden in the poem. He uses all the varying materials in his mind—" gold, silver and base lead "—to build a fabric, from one view a thing of surpassing beauty, from another fantastic and bizarre. In spite of all it is the peak of his achievement. It is the manifestation of his ideal, the glorification of the spiritual life which alone is real, and which alone gives meaning to the things of the material world.

The obvious story is as simple as it can be. With reminiscences of earlier study in his mind, and with Malory, Villemarqué and Michel as guides, Hawker gives the story of the events leading up to the knights' departure on the quest, but his authorities supply the mere framework ; the details are his own. It is to the speeches, the emblems of the knights, the visions that

---

[1] " Poems of Blake," Oxford edition, p. 197.
[2] " Life and Letters," p. 449.

we must look for Hawker's message, for, as we have already seen, the poem is an allegory to which the key is given by the identification of King Arthur with the author himself. The mediæval story of the quest of the Holy Grail, with its setting in history and its background of natural features, holds a spiritual lesson in just the same way as history and nature were for Hawker symbols of the world of reality. The knights represent the world ; those few who set out on the quest the Church of Christ. Arthur, symbolic of the priest, reminds them of the foundations of their faith, of the necessity for spiritual endurance, and of their ideal—the vision of God. But the vision is not for all, and with his love of embodying ancient legends and his usual spatial imagery, Hawker describes the varying degrees of vision under symbols of regions of the earth. " The Orient is the home of God." " The wide, wide West ; the imaged Zone of man." " The North ! the lair of demons," and " the happy South—the angel's home." The knights then represent the different qualities of spiritual life in Christian men. Lancelot with a wrongful earthly love tugging at his heart, goes out hampered on the quest, and will easily yield to the temptations to give it up—" his battle-foe, the demon —ghastly war ! " though by what forms he will be assailed, we shall never know, as Hawker wrote only the first four lines of the canto in which he intended to " trace Lord Lancelot's northward way." Tristan, with only Hope to urge him towards the goal, might win spiritual blessing if he could keep his heart pure, but he may stoop to strive for earthly rewards, and his hope will be degraded to a longing for earthly fame. Percival, with Faith to lead him on, will pass through the world surrounded by spiritual presences—" God's white army in their native Land," but only Galahad, the mystic, purified by the consuming power of Love, and so capable of apprehending Love, may win the Graal

Full filled and running o'er with Numynous light,
As though it held and shed the visible God.

So much of the plan of the whole poem we may gather from the one canto finished, but, while Hawker's chief subject is one outside the limits of Space and Time, he contrives by means of the visions called up by Merlin to give his views on the evolution of spiritual life in history, and flatters himself he has " succeeded best in modern history."[1] This, the most obscure part of the poem, is fully explained by references to it in his letters. " I hope you will like the Three Visions at the Close called up by Merlin for the King, The First—England under Arthur and His wars, Second the Saxon and Norman Times of Sangraal Light, Third from 1536 to 1863 with my notions of the Battle of Waterloo and the Armstrong Gun—Gas, Steam, Electric Telegraph."[2] Remembering his theory of the effect of the Reformation in England, and his views on scientific progress, we shall understand his references to the " troops of the demon-north " and their power, and hear in Merlin's last words to the King, the voice of a prophet calling to his countrymen to take a nobler view of life and to strive for a higher ideal.

> " Ah ! haughty England ! lady of the wave ! "
> Thus said pale Merlin to the listening king,
> " What is thy glory in the world of stars ?
> To scorch and slay : to win demoniac fame,
> In arts and arms ; and then to flash and die ! . . .
> Ah ! native England ! wake thine ancient cry :
> Ho ! for the Sangraal ! vanish'd Vase of Heaven,
> That held, like Christ's own heart, a hin of blood ! "[3]

" The Sangraal " is a fragment, but it is difficult to see how Hawker could have finished it. He had put all the stores of his mind into it, and his theme did not need to be developed further. The Quest of the Divine is not to be bound within the limits of Space and Time: he could not describe the end of the quest, and still preserve the allegory. The thought is complete, though the form is imperfect.

[1] " Life and Letters," p. 448.
[2] *Ibid.*, p. 446.
[3] " Cornish Ballads," p. 190.

But on the whole the study of Hawker's thought leaves a feeling of sadness in the mind. The story is one of wasted powers, and as such holds all the elements of tragedy, for when we come to assess the worth of his meditation as a contribution to human knowledge we find little of real value. It is too full of " infused remembrances " to be original, and too fragmentary and disconnected to be considered as a new setting of old material. Mystic after mystic through the centuries has reiterated the main articles of Hawker's creed : the transcendence and immanence of God, the symbolic value of the natural world, the reality of the spirit alone ; and their visions have been wider and deeper and fuller than his. Compared with the wisdom of Boehme or Blake, Hawker's vision is as minute as is the lamp of the glow-worm in proportion to the light of the sun. They connect thought and conduct in their systems of philosophy ; though Hawker does the same in his own life, his philosophical speculation and his teaching on life and conduct seem separate links in a chain which he seldom attempts to solder together. He lacks constructive power, and his thought is a collection of scraps. It is a heavy indictment, and under it Hawker appears a failure. He is not even able to take old thought and charge it with fresh inspiration, as William Law did when he set his own mark on the philosophy of Boehme. Most melancholy of all is the fact that he left unaccomplished the work which was waiting to be done, and which he alone could do.

We cannot blame his age for not hearing him, as we can blame the eighteenth century for ignoring Blake. The fault lies on his side, for he never raises his voice above a whisper. Though men who could turn deaf ears to the vehemence of Carlyle would doubtless have failed to hear Hawker if he had spoken out, we must admit that he never gave them the chance. And though he considers his notes " sentences of great value to future Scribes and Students of the Oracles of God,"[1]

[1] " Life and Letters," p. 327.

it is asking a good deal of posterity to expect them to
do the sorting and arranging of ideas which the writer
should do in his own mind. One cannot reap where
there has been no labour after sowing. It is another
manifestation of Hawker's vanity that he should expect it. But tragedy lies in his lack of achievement. It
is not laziness which makes him a failure. Like Ham-
let, he suffers from a fatal paralysis of the will, and his
energy loses itself in the quicksands of aimless speculation. His favourite comparison of the course of his
life to a waterfall is truer still of his thought. " It
bounds into the air like a broken purpose, and, caught
up and driven backward by the wind, it is shattered
into spray and lost."[1]

Yet though the potential energy is wasted, the
spray may refresh a weary traveller. Ineffective as
Hawker's meditation seems to have been, it was that
of a mystic, and as such he has his mite to offer to the
treasury of spiritual thought. The world can ill afford
to lose sight of any who have a message, however fal-
tering, which deals with the relative values of matter
and spirit. Hawker added something of his own to the
old theory when he evolved his idea of " Numyne."
He brought it up-to-date, and presented it in the form
most fitting for the age. What the Victorians needed
most was to be shown that religion and life were one,
and that every phase of human activity might be
sanctified. Hawker could do this only by bringing the
thoughts uppermost in men's minds into touch with
religion ; and as scientific discovery—in biology, geol-
ogy, physics, psychology—was the all-engrossing subject, he risked the danger of making " Numyne "
appear material in order to win the attention of those,
who in contemplation of matter had lost sight of spirit.
He leaves others to tackle the labour of bringing religion to bear on industrialism, on politics, on government, and seeks only to reconcile science and religion.
And where Tennyson was weak, Hawker was strong ;

[1] " Life and Letters," p. 195.

where Tennyson represented the doubts of his age,
Hawker stood away from his time, and saw each new
discovery not as an alarming catastrophe, but as another witness to the truth. And because we in the
twentieth century, though living in the midst of ter-
mendous discoveries, have not yet advanced as far as
Hawker in spiritual vision, his message has still its
work to do, and cannot lose its force while as a nation
we continue to set material luxury above spiritual
well-being.

The critical mind may see but this grain of living
seed among the chaff of Hawker's thought, but one
prejudiced in his favour could discover other virtues.
Of him, as truly as of Sir Thomas Browne, it may be
said that he " thought with his imagination,"[1] and
such minds are as interesting for their methods as for
the results of their speculation. Hawker's mind is like
a tangled forest, in which only one path leads to the
centre, but once on that road we cannot miss our way,
for every track that branches from it rejoins it further
on. Those who see no beauty in a mind that is not
logical and well-ordered will always be exasperated by
it, but for others its very disorder will create a certain
fascination. Such glaring contrasts, such extraordin-
ary juxtapositions, such a strange medley of fact and
fancy, yet capable of being resolved, as they are in the
Sangraal, into one harmonious whole by the force of
poetic imagination, cannot fail to attract those who
find a joy in unexpectedness and mystery. Diffuse,
unbalanced, prejudiced, as his thought often is, it
sometimes lights up dark places with startling clarity,
and is seldom without a strange beauty of its own. It
has the power itself of stirring imagination. Indeed,
the history of Hawker's thought might be compared
with that of the Graal legend which he so much loved.
The story had its birth in primitive nature-worship.
Hawker, first inspired by the beauty of nature, in-
corporated in his thought all the heritage of nature

[1] C. H. Herford, Preface—Everyman Edition, p. xiv.

superstition which he found flourishing among his
Cornish parishioners. The Graal legend acquired historical setting ; Hawker chose such a background for
much of his thought. The Graal legend took a religious
aspect, and became connected with the most sacred
events in the history of Christianity ; Hawker found
the culmination of his ideal in the Catholic Church.
Both the legend and Hawker lost in simplicity through
the accretion of mediæval beliefs, and in grandeur
through the touch of the nineteenth century. Perhaps
the hold that the Graal legend has on the imagination
of men may be prophetic of the future for Hawker's
thought, but it cannot be so unless he has also the
power of imaginative expression of the truths which
he has perceived " in paths of thought."

Although some of Hawker's pronouncements are
obscure, the meaning is never very deeply hidden. Of
course he had neither the visionary nor the intellectual
power to build up a symbolic system such as Blake's,
but the fact that his thought is easily unravelled does
not mean that it is petty. Only the man who has
thought clearly can write simply of great subjects, and
it is in that Hawker's greatness lies. It is his art to be
simple in expression, and therefore the study of
Hawker as thinker must be completed by that of
Hawker as artist.

CHAPTER V.

HAWKER AS ARTIST.

MEMORY and Imagination—two of man's mightiest powers—Hawker possessed in large measure. They were but unprofitable servants to him as thinker, for the one kept in his mind old searchings after truth, and the other led him through a barren land peopled with strange shapes, but in his work as artist they were above price. By their help Hawker takes a high place as a craftsman. Memory supplies a fading view or a dying refrain, and Imagination plays on it, and makes the conception its own. As few of Hawker's ideas were original in themselves, but became so through his treatment or in the setting he gave them, it follows that form and style in his work are of great importance. His true method of expression, then, is his poetry, where an imaginative conception may be clothed in fitting language, but when he lacked both energy and time to write poetry, and fell back on jotted notes or prose articles, the style sometimes tends to overwhelm the matter.

For better or worse, Hawker had the artistic temperament. That being so, he could not help studying the effect of his self-expression—an attitude, which, when directed towards his own personality, laid him open to the charge of playing a part. In his work it made him consider style of equal importance with thought. In his medium of language he was both painter and musician, using words sometimes as strokes of the brush, sometimes as notes in a chord.

We have already seen his power of visual imagina-

I

tion used to present abstract and hypothetical ideas, but the deliberate artist is seen at work most clearly in a description of a past scene, which was printed in " Willis's Current Notes " in May 1855. Hawker reconstructs the scene recorded in St. John VII., 37, giving in the last paragraph the details which he would depict if he were a painter, but showing himself in his first description the literary artist. " There then stood Jesu, around Him the twelve men, the bearded Bishops of his future Church. The columns and the Court were wreathed with bowers of green branches, from the patient palm-tree with its turbaned brow, and the willows of the watercourses, which in those days grew upright, but which after their rods had been taken to scourge the Lord withal, drooped evermore in memorial grief, the citron bough, heavy with fruit and the myrtle tree. All at once there was the shout of the trumpet, and a loud and lifted Psalm ; it is that Ode which is now read as the twelfth chapter of the book of Isaiah. The Levites draw near, and a procession enters in solemn array. They have drawn water from the brook of Siloam, which flows fast by the Oracle of God. A priest bears it in a golden vase, and they pass on to pour it as their usage was on the altar of holocaust—$\pi\rho\hat{\omega}\tau o\nu$ $\mu\grave{\epsilon}\nu$ $\H{\upsilon}\delta\omega\rho$, *i.e.*, water was first. They have passed through the cloister of the men, and as their voices fade into the inner sanctuary, a deep and solemn tone proclaims in thrilling words— ' If any man thirst, let him come unto Me and drink !'[1] And lest any should complain that irrelevant details and unwieldy sentences detract from its artistic beauty, it may be added that Hawker himself called it " rudis indigestaque moles," and declares he would " have written with more coherence and care,"[2] if he had known it was for print. Yet though we may see Hawker here as the conscious artist, his pictures are never drawn for their own sake alone. They are creat-

---

[1] Quoted in " Life and Letters," p. 257.
[2] " Life and Letters," p. 256.

ed with a definite purpose, and Hawker's art is the handmaid of his religion. He remarks in his notes, "How graphic was all the instruction of Jesus Christ,"[1] and following his Master, he uses his power of calling up a picture only to teach. This didactic purpose prevents it from being a characteristic of his poetry, when his artistic instinct is strongest. We shall look in vain in his verse for pictures as clearly drawn as that of the scene of the Annunciation or of the walk " on the Path between the vines " of " The Mother and Her Son,"[2] which appear in his notes, and one of which was definitely intended for a sermon. There are a few lightly-sketched " scenes of the former men " in the early poems where he is still interested in the past, there are the visions of King Arthur in " The Quest," where the poet wishes to instruct, but no descriptions where every detail aids the conception of beauty, no passages which exist for the sake of their intrinsic loveliness alone. Hawker's quest of Beauty was not that of Keats or Tennyson. No passage shows this more clearly than the description of the scene " in Arthur's Hall," before the knights set out on the quest.

> They meet for solemn severance, knight and king,
> Where gate and bulwark darken o'er the sea.
> Strong man for meat, and warriors at the wine,
> They wreak the wrath of hunger on the beeves,
> They rend rich morsels from the savoury deer,
> And quench the flagon like Brun-guillie dew!
> Hear! how the minstrels prophesy in sound,
> Shout the King's Waes-hael, and Drink-hael the Queen!
> Then said Sir Kay, he of the arrowy tongue,
> " Joseph and Pharaoh! how they build their bones!
> Happier the boar were quick than dead to-day."
>
> The Queen! The Queen! how haughty on the dais!
> The sunset tangled in her golden hair:
> A dove amid the eagles—Guennivar!
> Aishah! what might is in that glorious eye!

---

[1] " Stones Broken from the Rocks," p. 108.
[2] Ibid., pp. 15, 16.

See their tamed lion from Brocelian's glade,
Couched on the granite like a captive king !
A word—a gesture—or a mute caress—
How fiercely fond he droops his billowy mane,
And wooes with tawny lip, his lady's hand !

The dawn is deep ; the mountains yearn for day ;
The hooting cairn is husht—that fiendish noise,
Yelled from the utterance of the rending rock,
When the fierce dog of Cain barks from the moon.

The bird of judgment chants the doom of night.
The billows laugh a welcome to the day,
And Camlan ripples, seaward, with a smile.[1]

The picture is drawn, but in outline only. There is no background and no detail. We see the knights feasting —Sir Kay—the minstrels—just roughly drafted. One other figure has received a few distinguishing touches —the Queen, fondling the tamed lion, is glorious in the beauty of her hair and eyes. Yet we have a vivid impression of the scene, but the reason is that it is persented to us as from the stage of a theatre, and not on the curtain of a cinematograph. Sound must play its part too, and there is no lack of it in the description.

Hark ! stern Dundagel softens into song !

The minstrels play, the knights sing their " Waeshael," Sir Kay mutters his biting words. The silence of night falls, broken only by the crowing of the cock as day breaks, and by the ripple of ocean and stream. Hawker's art is that of the musician rather than of the painter, and he makes his effect through the sense of hearing rather than of sight. His poetry is adorned by few pictures, but it is a " stately pleasure-dome " full of sweet sounds.

The description of the banquet is typical of many others. Even if we turn to poems which have left the impression of scenes from the past, we shall find it is to sounds we are bidden to listen, often with Hawker's

[1] " Cornish Ballads," p. 181.

irritating exclamations, " Hark ! " or " Hear ! " The
Minster of the Trees is

> the cloister lowly laid
> Where pacing monks at solemn evening made
> Their chanted orisons ; and as the breeze
> Came up the vale, by rock and tree delay'd,
> They heard the awful voice of many seas
> Blend with thy pausing hymn—Thou Minster of the Trees.[1]

The kernel of the next two verses is in each case a
sound. The poet's record of " vision and dream " in
" Home Once More " ends with that of " gesture and
tone of saintly Paul,

> Till fancy heard the iron bands
> That shook upon his lifted hands.[2]

The sounds of nature form a mighty chorus in his
verse—the howling of the storm in winter, the sighing
of a summer breeze, the beating of the waves, the
singing of the brooks, the harsh call of the curlew or
raven, the cry of the cuckoo, the sweet note of the
robin or linnet—all play their part. Brought before
our minds by echo or description, they testify to the
poet's sensitive ear. Like De Quincey, he thought that
the πόντιων τε κυματων ανηριθμον γέλασμα of Æschylus
referred to sound, though he imagined his idea quite
original, for when he suggested it to Tennyson, " I was
glad to find," he tells us, " that he half agreed with a
thought I have long cherished, that these words relate
to the *Ear* and not to the *Eye*. He did not disdain a
version of mine made long ago :—

> Hark how old Ocean laughs with all his waves."[3]

As thrilling as natural music is the peal of the church
bells, while most wonderful of all are the words of men.
Poem after poem is framed for the human voice as expressive of some emotion or desire of man. Hymns,
carols, dirges, war-songs and folk-songs follow hard on

[1] " Cornish Ballads," p. 42.
[2] *Ibid.*, p. 60.
[3] " Life and Letters," p. 190.

one another, while poems like " The Baptism of the
Peasant and the Prince " or " The Lady's Well " are
utterances of the voice of speech rather than of song.
" Isha Cherioth " and the " Nun of Carmel " are presented to us merely by their words. " A language is a
Man,"[1] Hawker writes in his note-books, and his interest in personality fastened on its means of expression. Language became his diversion.

In his love of words Hawker is very much like Sir
Thomas Browne, a writer whom he must have appreciated, though the only sign he gives of knowing him
is a quotation in the notes. He has the same delight in
coining words of his own, words of as little use to the
language as many of Browne's. " I say, cometicized,
that is, acted on by the approaching comet,"[2] he
writes in 1857, and instead of the word, " engraving,"
substitutes " carvure " with the remark, " If no such
word, it is time there should be. I invent it."[3] In the
notes we find " the burthen or Everphone (R.S.H.'s
word) or chorus," to show us how little of the scientific
attitude there was in his interest in words. They did
not attract Hawker in the same way as they did his
neighbour, William Barnes though he does occasionally consider derivations. He was fascinated by their
power of suggestion, their music, their mystery, and
he treated them as a collector does his treasures.
" Names," he writes in the notes, " a sweeping sound
—a full peal of bells, and some swing up from the
abyss of time as though they had brooded over the
ancient glory there."[4] His favourites were those which
had beauty of sound, but some he valued for their age,
and he delighted in discovering hidden meaning, in
rubbing up dull ones, and in comparing late specimens
with earlier ones.

We need only turn to " The Quest of the Sangraal "
to see him at work—or is it not rather, at play ! Why

[1] Unpublished notes.
[2] " Life and Letters," p. 296.
[3] *Ibid.*, p. 265.
[4] Unpublished.

" a hin of blood " in the second line, except that the
word fitted both for association, as the note explains,
and for alliterative sound ? Why " an aumry chest "
to hold Merlin's prophecy but that the word has a history : " it is the breviate of Almeries for Aumoire (I
think) and meant originally what we call Alms-Chest
or *perhaps* Archive, or *vulgo* Cupboard."[1] Why " lib-
bard " instead of " leopard " " to mark the Norman
period of History " in the second vision, but that the
older word fits into the music of the line ? Igdrasil,
Raun, Waes-hael, Orison, Anathema ! Maran-atha !
Aishah ! a strange company, but each word is dear to
him for history or sound, and the crown is given to
Hebrew for its mystery by his use of it for the words
" hewn by Merlin on a runic stone :—Kirioth el Zan-
nah aulohee pedah." One of his notes throws light on
his attitude towards this tongue. " In what language
did the Family at Nazareth converse ? " he asks, and
answers it thus. " Surely in the Syrian Hebrew, the
oldest vernacular, the Mother Tongue of the Angels,
the Channel of the Messages, the direct echo of God's
own Memra."[2] That it is the sound and not the appearance of the word that matters to him is shown by the
footnotes to the two Hebrew words in later poems.
" The Fatal Ship " contains the words " Lord Yahvah
of the Waters ! " with the note, " ' Yahvah,' the
Hebrew name of God the Trinity, wrongly spelt and
pronounced ' Jehovah,' "[3] and the poem, " $\dot{\epsilon}\nu$ $\dot{\alpha}\rho\chi\eta$,"
shows us that the word, " aulohee," above is Hawker's
own phonetic spelling of the Hebrew, " Elohim."[4]

The appeal of words to his imagination is shown no-
where more clearly than in a letter of 1857 where he
mentions " the Buddhist Formulary," and continues,
" the Total Creed of the largest Share of Mankind this
very day, only Six Syllables and Four Words. All
through Hindustan, Thibet, Tartary, China, carved

[1] " Life and Letters," p. 434.
[2] " Stones Broken from the Rocks," p. 18.
[3] " Cornish Ballads," p. 206.
[4] *Ibid.*, p. 298.

on Altars, woven into Tapestry, painted over Tombs,
chanted by myriads, taught to children and Men,
sounded in Prayer, proclaimed by Lama and Priest as
an embodiment of all Human Knowledge and Divine
Revelation. Here it is in my Autograph

Om = Mani = Padmi = om

pronounced oūm mănnĭ Pādmĭ oūm ... It is no more
—no less than the Gasp of many Lands—the agony of
Nations in their Prayer—an unfulfilled entreaty—as
it were the Echo of a Hope denied. O ! in the sense of
Utinam ! ' O for '—or, ' O that I could win '—or, ' O
that I had not lost.' O ! for the Jewel of the Lotus . . .¹
a vast multitude in this utterance of pleading anguish
is a sound so woebegone that few can hear it without
tears, altho' they know not the meaning of the Voice."²

Hawker's sensitiveness to sound had a two-fold
effect on his work—on form and on style. For him, as
for Mr. Yeats, a word was a living thing, and the written word but a poor makeshift for that formed by the
breath of man. In a book the runes rest " couching
like slumbering birds. Your voice embodies them with
sudden rushing life," we find in the notes, and again,
" It is *not* in type, it is not in the printed page whereby
men teach and learn, but it is by the channel of the
voice and ear."³ With this ideal what place was there
for him as a poet in modern civilisation, where for all
practical purposes he must depend on the printed page
—in an epoch when " of making many books there is
no end ? " He was no poet of the study, content to
draw on the stores of his own mind to provide reading
matter for an unseen public, and careless of their
opinion—hence those barren years of middle age. In
his art he belonged to the years before printing ; in
him the " scop " of Anglo-Saxon times lived again. If
he had been able to chant his verses straight to the
hearts of the listeners, his biographer would have had

¹ Part of letter missing.
² " Life and Letters," p. 368.
³ Unpublished.

no need to find excuses for the small quantity of his work. As it was, he felt himself baffled because he could not get into personal touch with his audience, and one of his apparent eccentricities is simply an attempt to overcome this obstacle. Many of his poems were printed in leaflet form, and distributed among his parishioners, and a letter of 1861 describes an effort to give them wider circulation without losing the personal effect. He writes, " I have at last discovered a mode of publicity and circulation whereby I baffle the resolve of these Editors that nobody shall read my lines. It is a costly but effectual plan. I print my verses at my own expense in London, get down some hundreds on fly-leaves like " The Comet " and then insert a copy or two ingeniously in letters of business when I pay an account or transmit any formal envelope, and thus my lines in a moment of surprise or curiosity *are* read and *do* become known."[1] No doubt the majority went straight into the wastepaper-basket, but Hawker had done his best. Both his mysticism and his art demanded hearers, and those his poetry failed to attract.

There was, however, another avenue of expression open to Hawker in which both mysticism and art could have free play. Though his sermons were inspired, guided and controlled by his mystic outlook, there can be no doubt that Hawker was an artist in the field of religious oratory. Descriptions of his preaching show the part his own personality played, and probably only the fact that, as always, his mysticism dominated his art, prevented him from being famous as a preacher. He writes in the notes, " If a man have a gift (sc. of eloquence) and be forbidden room to reveal it here it is meant to be revealed in Paradise," and in a letter after a successful sermon thinks " it proves I could have preached *if I had been allowed*." We are told that " Hawker was a wonderful preacher. People came from miles around to hear him,"[2] and

[1] Quoted in Introduction to " Cornish Ballads," p. vii.
[2] Note by C. E. Byles, " Stones Broken from the Rocks," p. 110.

Dr. Lee, speaking of one of the sermons he preached in London at All Saints, Lambeth, to earn money for the restoration of Morwenstow Church, writes, " His Sermon I shall never forget. He spoke most eloquently of the certainty of the Resurrection, of the Faith and the Hope and the Joy of the Mother of God, and of the blessed end of our own enduring warfare here. His voice, melodious, and of a wide compass, was as clear as a bell ; his manner simple, dignified and loving ; his oratory perfect. The congregation listened with breathless attention, and were deeply struck by his remarkable powers."[1] Hawker's comments on this success only show that his own attitude is the same as when he wrote in 1862, " What pleasure can there be on one's Bed of Death, to remember a fine discourse or the applause of a multitude in comparison with the noiseless delight of peacemaking and loving-kindness to the Poor in Spirit whom the Master loves ? "[2] He gives his views more fully in 1864. " I have had all my life a horror of Shew Sermons—that is to say of a Man's getting up to preach a fine discourse to win admiration. We should always ask ' what is our mission ? ' Mine is to teach my own people."[3]

But even with this ideal Hawker might have won a place beside Jeremy Taylor, who is hailed as man of letters by virtue of his sermons alone. He has something of the same equipment, and the fact that Hawker addressed a less cultured audience would not have made his sermons any the less works of art. But neither mysticism nor art demanded their preservation. " Christ never took a pen in His hand, nor dipped in ink. On the contrary, His *tongue* was the *pen* of the ready writer,"[4] we find jotted in the notes, and as the artist in Hawker considered the sermon as a spoken thing, most of his later ones were delivered extempore and never written down, and his early MS.

[1] " Life and Letters," p. 612.
[2] *Ibid.*, p. 355.
[3] *Ibid.*, p. 485.
[4] " Stones Broken from the Rocks," p. 81.

ones burnt. Except for a few special ones which have survived, we can only guess at what they were like, from some of his notes and some of the rules by which he was guided.

He often mentions the subjects in letters. " I preached to-day on the image of Caesar graven on his coin, and on the Image of God imprinted upon the Face of Adam, and by him debased." Nov. 15th, 1857.[1] " I preached to-day from the Gospel, ' Gather up the fragments that remain that nothing be lost —' and meaning that the bread which our Lord had touched and blessed was not to be trodden under foot and treated with disrespect, but to be honoured and treasured as the hallowed gift of God. Whereas, when wheat was low in price a year ago, many Farmers here gave it to their swine—a sin for which they now are punished." March 18th, 1860.[2] " To-day the Gospel of the Birds and the Flowers. Our Lord on Mount Tabor with the fed multitudes grouped in the distance, the Syrian Farmers at the foot of the Hill—Clusters of flowers between the Rocks, Birds gliding to and fro. So He called on the people to choose their World— which of the twain, etc." September 13th, 1863.[3] There was very often the ingenuity of art in his choice of a text to fit a special occasion, but mysticism dictated its development. " When you are about to treat a theme ask yourself what on such a subject and at such a time and to such an audience would *He* have said."[4] He saw the temptation open to all speakers with power to touch the hearts of men, and noted, " All attempts at emotion except through the reason fanatical and sectarian. Our blessed Saviour did not."[5] He had decided views on exposition. " A Sermon should never say : This *may* mean so and so, but say (after due search) This *means*. There is no real ' may

1 " Life and Letters," p. 304.
2 *Ibid.*, p. 323.
3 *Ibid.*, p. 431.
4 " Stones Broken from the Rocks," p. 110.
5 *Ibid.*, p. 109.

be ' in Holy Writ." " Even the language of persuasion seems misplaced in the enforcement of Holy Truth. It is like recommending Wares for Sale. A mere enunciation of sacred facts, without anticipation of the possibility of disbelief appears to me the most adapted to the Words of God. A simple oracular communication is best."[1]

As for style, there the artist finds support in his mysticism for his own desire. " The Founder of our Faith breathed the Inspiration of Heaven in the very poetry of prose . . . It was with the elegance of human taste that the Great Prophet decorated His doctrines with metaphor and similitude. It was the consecration of eloquence that the Saviour of Man interwove the graces of human rhetoric in the language of God."[2] With such a precedent Hawker had no hesitation in bringing all his powers of imagination and memory to bear on his style, and the sermons which remain show his feeling for words, his arresting use of imagery, his power of allusion. But there can be no doubt that Hawker's description of Newman, as " Orator more than Reasoner,"[3] was even truer of himself, and works of art as his sermons no doubt were in their delivery, they would not have passed through the ordeal of print with so little hurt as Jeremy Taylor's. What would be the effect in an ordered dissertation of such a guiding rule as the following : " Rhetoric. For a pulpit. Must not condense but amplify. More words than necessary must be used, for the people are slow to apprehend " ?[4] Only in his poetry is Hawker the true artist in style, for the devices of rhetoric have crept into all his prose written for publication, and entirely fitting though they may be in impassioned oratory, they are but meretricious adornments to descriptions of scenery or simple narrative.

Hawker's prose is represented by his letters, notes,

[1] " Stones Broken from the Rocks," p. 110.
[2] *Ibid.*, p. 107.
[3] *Ibid.*, p. 95.
[4] *Ibid.*, p. 112.

and scattered articles to magazines, ranging in length
from a single paragraph to the narrative and descriptive pieces now collected under the title, " Footprints
of Former Men in Far Cornwall." The latter are the
only ones which have any claim to be considered as
literary forms, and though of little real value, they are
not without interest. For the weakness which affects
them all is one which rarely appears in Hawker's
poetry. They are burdened with self-esteem, and are
therefore artificial, and to a certain extent, insincere.
We could almost guess from their tone that the writer
was striving to attract attention, if we did not know
from the story of his life that they were mere pot-
boilers. We cannot judge Hawker harshly, for they
seemed to him the only means by which he could earn
a much-needed income to support the wife and children of his old age. He showed in his first book of poems
that he knew the ballad to be a finer mould in which
to cast impressions of romantic Cornish worthies than
a rambling and inflated narrative, while the article on
" Morwenstow " is merely a prose rendering of the
theme of " Morwennae Statio," and a vehicle for in-
troducing four of his other poems to the public. His
prose works add little to his fame as an artist. There is
small evidence of the activity of his imagination, except in the re-arrangement of material in the story of
the Botathen Ghost and the additions to the story of
Daniel Gumb.

But unoriginal and affected as these writings are,
they are interesting, because in them the spirit of the
seventeenth century seems to meet that of the nineteenth. With all the panoply of romance which is at
his command as the disciple of Scott, Hawker seems to
be giving the history of his county of Cornwall in the
same way as men of an earlier time tried to tell the
history of England. He writes the stories of Daniel
Gumb, of Antony Payne, of Black John, of Cruel
Coppinger with the same mental background and the
same aim as the character-writers of the seventeenth

century. He too has been nourished on North and
Philemon Holland ; he too wishes to show what manner of men once lived. And when he gives the seventeenth century atmosphere unalloyed we see art tri-
umphant. In the letter supposed to have been written
by Antony Payne to his mistress, Lady Grace, to announce the death of Sir Beville Granville at the battle
of Lansdown, Hawker's use of prose justifies itself.
With his quaint whimsy he makes it appear the work
of another, and the suppression of his own personality
allows imagination to take its rightful place. We cannot doubt that it is Hawker's own invention, for
Antony Payne, though " happy in his language and of
such a ready wit that he was called . . . the Falstaff of
the West "[1] was surely a man of deeds rather than of
words, and there is no hint that he was a poet with
power to reach the sublime. Besides, Hawker's own
love of words gives him away ; no seventeenth century
retainer would have used the word ' trothful.' The
simplicity of this letter is Hawker's greatest achievement in prose, and we shall later see the same gift in
his poetry. " Thus it ran :

HONOURED MADAM,—Ill news flieth apace. The heavy tidings no
doubt hath already travelled to Stowe that we have lost our
blessed master by the enemy's advantage. You must not, dear lady,
grieve too much for your noble spouse. You know, as we all believe,
that his soul was in heaven before his bones were cold. He fell, as he
did often tell us he wished to die, in the great Stuart cause, for his
country and his king. He delivered to me his last commands, and
with such tender words for you and for his children as are not to be
set down with my poor pen, but must come to your ears upon my
best heart's breath. Master John, when I mounted him on his
father's horse, rode him into the war like a young prince, as he is,
and our men followed him with their swords drawn and with tears
in their eyes. They did say they would kill a rebel for every hair of
Sir Beville's beard. But I bade them remember their good master's
word, when he wiped his sword after Stamford fight ; how he said,
when their cry was, ' Stab and Slay ! ' ' Halt, men ! God will
avenge ! ' I am coming down with the mournfullest load that ever
a poor servant did bear, to bring the great heart that is cold to

[1] " Footprints," p. 113.

Kilkhampton vault. Oh, my lady, how shall I ever brook your weeping face ? But I will be trothful to the living and to the dead.

These, honoured madam, from thy saddest, truest servant,
ANTONY PAYNE."[1]

Hawker's prose style is like the man himself—fascinating, yet at times most exasperating. He was a poet through and through, and when he writes prose, he is working unfamiliar metal. He cannot help trying to make an effect even when he is stating simple fact. The result is that he can describe a pitch-pipe as follows : "This is an instrument of very remote antiquity. It was used in Greek and Roman oratory to suggest the rise and fall of the pleader's voice. It was adopted to fulfil the self-same office in ecclesiastical eloquence ; and the voices of St. Augustine and St. Chrysostom were roused or subdued by the τοναριον, in accordance with the size of the structure, or the extent of the audience. It is to be lamented that modern oratory is devoid of such an excellent means of modulation, and that the usage of the pipe . . . is limited as in Morwenstow, to rural choirs in remote Churches."[2] Even more over-weighted is the account of the roof of Morwenstow Church, for it has to carry along with it the self-satisfaction of the writer who has gained his point.[3] "Shingles of rended oak occupy the place of the usual, but far more recent, tiles which cover other churches ; and it is not a little illustrative of the antique usages of this remote and lonely sanctuary that no change has been wrought in the long lapse of ages, in this unique and costly, but fit and durable, roofing. It supplies a singular illustration of the Syriac version of the 90th Psalm, wherein, with prophetic reference to these commemorations of the death-bed of the Messias, it is written, ' Lord, Thou hast been our roof from generation to generation.' "[4] And this from the man who

[1] " Footprints," p. 117.
[2] " Antiquities in E. and S. Cornwall," J. T. Blight, 1858, p. 117.
[3] V. Chapter III., ante, pp. 61, 62.
[4] " Footprints," p. 20.

condemned the use of " twenty epithets for a single noun," and said, " If I may not call a spade a spade I cannot write at all ! "[1]

Hawker considered himself a judge of prose, but his standards were out-of-date. In nothing is he more old-fashioned than in his prose. It is full of reminiscences, and lacks the alert quality which we demand in good modern prose writing. Its foundation is the sixteenth century language of the Prayer-book and the seventeenth century language of the Authorised Version, but Hawker's memory was of such a kind that it was always presenting fit quotations from any of the writings with which his mind was stored. Like De Quincey, he was ever on the look-out for analogies ; but for the one, prose was the highest form of expression, for Hawker only the second-best. He needed the restraint of poetry to produce his best ; it was, as for Donne, his true means of expression. Very rarely is his prose simple ; even in his letters there is constant allusion and quotation, and it can be called good only when the subject is one fitly treated in poetic prose. Yet in spite of its patchwork composition, the effect is satisfying, for it is original, and in one sense, good style, in that it exactly expresses the man. He tries to carry out his own definition of " Eloquence " by writing " Noble and Natural thoughts . . . in graphic and graceful language," and certainly does sometimes succeed in making " a notch in the memory," and in writing " phrases to fascinate and instruct future generations."[2]

His originality appears in his prose in vividness of metaphor and simile. Much of the charm of his letters comes from his power of graphic illustration. St. Thomas Aquinas is " the Hive of the World's Honey of all ages,"[3] England is " a large Blaspheming Smithery,"[4] Pusey has " a woolly mind,"[5] and a friend

---

[1] " Life and Letters," p. 514.　　　[4] *Ibid.*, p. 240.
[2] *Ibid.*, p. 539.　　　　　　　　　 [5] *Ibid.*, p. 518.
[3] *Ibid.*, p. 239.

is nicknamed the " Eiderdown."[1] These are the lowest
rungs of the ladder of imagination ; on a different
plane are the metaphors which give life to intangible
things. " Bad Bodily Health and a Deep Depression
of Mind are the two Warders that keep the Door of
my Earthly Existence ; "[2] " Sorrows hard and heavy
as the Nether Millstone; "[3] these are a little higher, but
above them we find such as:—" Prayer is the Key in the
Lock of God's promises,"[4] and reach the summit with a
jotting from the MS. notes, perfect in sublimity of
thought and beauty of expression: "Worship. A state of
calm and simple thought rippled with silent prayer."[5]
These scattered thoughts are like sparks revealing the
fire still living within though the steady light is
quenched. They show that Hawker had one of the
essential qualities of a great poet—the power " to
make the particular a symbol of the universal,"[6] and
they strike us all the more forcibly because the setting
is prose. In the poems our desire for the kindling word
is lulled by the symbolism of the main idea, and our
emotions and intellects are satisfied by the imaginative
conception as a whole rather than by its details. Only
in the later poems can figures be detached from their
context, and beautiful as they are in themselves, they
point to decadence.

Hawker, however, had ready to his hand a means of
decoration which was more to him even than metaphor.
He had learnt from the Authorised Version the beauty
of sound as well as of graphic expression. He had
learnt that comparisons might be emphasized by the
repetition of sound. Some of the metaphors in the
letters show this. Speaking of his poverty, he says,
" Besides all other goads there is the dull daily drop
that wears out the soul with low mean degrading

---

[1] Postscript to unpublished letter.
[2] " Life and Letters," p. 366.
[3] *Ibid.*, p. 598.
[4] *Ibid.*, p. 523.
[5] " Stones Broken from the Rocks," p. 106.
[6] Middleton Murry, " Problem of Style," p. 93.

K

money fears,"[1] and later, speaks of "the low base mean teeth that gnaw at the roots of my weary existence." But this very delight in the echoing word was a snare to him in his prose writing. As his critical power waned, he became more and more enthralled by sound. In prose, it appears in the use of alliteration and assonance to an extent only proper in poetry; in verse, by the use of special words or phrases for their sound alone. Is not the decoration in the following sentence out of all proportion to its subject ? " It became one of the usages among the graphic imagery of interior decoration to depict the heretic as mocking the mysteries with that glare of derision and gesture of disdain which admonish and instruct."[2] But all words with a vowel sound following the consonants ' gl ' had a fascination for him. " Glare," " gleam," " glide," " glow," " glory," occur again and again. In " The Fatal Ship," " The Monsters of the sea will glide and glare ; " in " Aurora," it is " the wild flames that glide and glare on high." In the fragment on " The Pelican" we find, " Ye will grow and glide in glory," and of Lady Grace it is said, " she will glide and she will gleam again." The Sangraal offers its example, " Will the glory gleam ? "

He could not resist the temptation to play on the sound of ' s.' Even in prose we find the following : " To withhold succour from the sea-man struggling with the sea ; "[3] and, " It had the sombre aspect of age and solitude, and looked the very scene of strange and supernatural events;"[4] and again, " the grooved pillars of solid or of a single stone in succeeding styles of architecture ; "[5] but in the poetry we may see alliteration done to death in the line in " Baal-Zephon : " " Sound the stern signal ! Summon sea and shore." Hawker used the ' s ' sound for no onomatopœic purpose, but

1 " Life and Letters," p. 365.
2 " Footprints," p. 11.
3 Ibid., p. 49.
4 Ibid., p. 163.
5 Ibid,. p. 10.

for sheer love of it ; he has his pet words, and forces them into the strangest contexts. We find, " the shuddering seer," " the shuddering sign," " the shuddering sepulchre," or again, " the seething sea," " the seething surges." He plays on different forms of the word " sever "—" severing seas," " severed souls," " severed shapes," "severed side," "solemn severance;" and " semblance " is another favourite—" semblance of a soul," " stern semblance." But this same fault of taste should lead us to look at the growth of that power which we see here falling into decay.

Hawker's use of alliteration and assonance is one of his most marked characteristics. He began the practice of it very early ; " David's Lament " in " Tendrils " is no mere paraphrase of " The Song of the Bow," but a different musical setting for the dirge, and though the poet is still inexperienced, it is easy to see he has learnt the value of vowel-sounds.

> From the borders of Judah let gladness be banish'd,
>   Ye maidens of Israel be deep in your woe.
> For the pride of the mighty in battle is vanish'd,
>   The chief of the sword, and the lord of the bow.[1]

The poem, " Clovelly," of 1825, shows his first steps in the art of alliteration, and points to Byron as his teacher. The favourite sounds of his old age were those of his youth—witness the lines,

> Dark sails that gleam on Ocean's heaving breast
> From the glad fisher-barks that homeward glide,
> To make Clovelly's shores at pleasant evening-tide.

And in the next verse :

> And ever and anon the impatient shock
>   Of some strong billow on the sounding shore.[2]

By the volume of 1832 he has acquired the master's

---

[1] " Cornish Ballads," p. 279.
[2] *Ibid.*, p. 3.

touch. The magic of " Featherstone's Doom " is in its
music.

> Twist thou and twine ! in light and gloom
>   A spell is on thy hand ;
> The wind shall be thy changeful loom,
>   Thy web the shifting sand.
>
> Twine from this hour in ceaseless toil,
>   On Blackrock's sullen shore ;
> Till cordage of the sand shall coil
>   Where crested surges roar.
>
> 'Tis for that hour, when, from the wave,
>   Near voices wildly cried,
> When thy stern hand no succour gave,
>   The cable at thy side.
>
> Twist thou and twine ! in light and gloom
>   The spell is on thine hand ;
> The wind shall be thy changeful loom,
>   Thy web the shifting sand ! [1]

He uses both vowel and consonant music for the purposes of onomatopœia in the last verse of " The Bells
of Bottreaux."

> Still when the storm of Bottreaux waves
> Is wakening in his weedy caves :
> Those bells, that sullen surges hide,
> Peal their deep notes beneath the tide :
>   " Come to thy God in time ! "
> Thus saith the ocean chime :
>   " Storm, billow, whirlwind past,
> Come to thy God at last ! " [2]

He finds this music sufficient ornament for his record
of mystic experience "at the foot of Rocky Carradon,"
the only lines from 1832 until " The Sangraal " of
1863, in which rhyme finds no place.

As he progresses, his art becomes less obvious. The
vowel-music is more subtle, the alliteration less in-

[1] " Cornish Ballads," p. 15.
[2] *Ibid.*, p. 18.

sistent. Only in the first verse of " The Sea-bird's Cry"
is it thrust at the reader, and the fact that the most
carefully constructed poem of the 1836 volume is the
most apparently simple one shows that Hawker has
learnt the secret of the art which hides art. The words
of the first verse of " The Cornish Mother's Lament "
are almost without exception of one syllable only, yet
what an added depth of sorrow is expressed by the alliteration of the mournful consonants *m* and *b*, and
the repeated *s* of the first line is like the indrawn
breath of a sob.

> They say 'tis a sin to sorrow—
>   That which God does is best :
> But 'tis only a month to-morrow,
>   I buried it from my breast.[1]

By 1840 Hawker had everything at his finger-tips.
He knew the value of simplicity, and the best means
of attaining it ; he knew the methods of decoration,
and had power to keep his love of it within bounds.
So in " Ecclesia " we see his art at its highest. The
grandeur of the raging sea demands an echoing music,
and we are given such a verse as the following :

> Mark where they writhe with pride and shame
> Fierce valour and the zeal of fame !
> Hear how their din of madness raves,
> The baffled army of the waves ! [2]

The poet wishes to bring before our imagination a
scene where all is peace, and his very words have a
soothing effect.

> A source of gentle waters, mute and mild,
>   A few calm reeds around the sedgy brink,
> The loneliest bird, that flees to waste or wild,
>   Might fold its feathers here in peace to drink.[3]

[1] " Cornish Ballads," p. 80.
[2] *Ibid.*, p. 69.
[3] *Ibid.*, p. 88.

Sometimes he uses it for emphasis alone, as in the last verse of " Morwennae Statio."

> Still points the tower, and pleads the bell ;
>   The solemn arches breathe in stone ;
> Window and wall have lips to tell
>   The mighty faith of days unknown.
> Yea ! flood and breeze and battle-shock
>   Shall beat upon this church in vain :
> She stands, a daughter of the rock,
>   The changeless God's eternal fane.[1]

Sometimes he had a double aim. The third and fourth verses of " ' I am the Resurrection and the Life ! ' saith the Lord," show alliteration used for echo and for emphasis.

> " Ashes to ashes—dust to dust "—
> The last farewell we sadly said.
> Our mighty hope—our certain trust—
> The resurrection of the dead.
>   Again all air, it glides around,
>   A voice ! the spirit of a sound.
>
> A doctrine dwells in that deep tone ;
> A truth is borne on yonder wing ;
> Long years ! long years ! the note is known—
> The blessed messenger of spring !
>   Thus saith that pilgrim of the skies :
>   " Lo ! all which dieth shall arise ! "[2]

And again we find it used to intensify sorrow, and yet in no way detracting from simplicity of expression. The maid who loved Iscariot mourns for the traitor.

> They say his sin was dark and deep,
>   Men shudder at his name—
> They spurn at me because I weep,
>   They call my sorrow, shame . . .
>
> .   .   .   .   .
>
> They tell of treachery bought and sold—
>   Perchance their words be truth—
> I only see the scenes of old ;
>   I hear his voice in youth.[3]

[1] " Cornish Ballads," p. 49.
[2] *Ibid.*, p. 55.
[3] *Ibid.*, p. 103.

It plays its part in one of the most perfect of Hawker's poems, " A Christ-Cross Rhyme " of 1845.

> Christ His Cross shall be my speed.
> Teach me, Father John, to read ;
> That in church on holy day
> I may chant the psalms and pray.
>
> Let me learn, that I may know
> What the shining windows show :
> Where the Lovely Lady stands
> With that bright Child in her hands
>
> Teach me letters, A, B, C,
> Till that I shall able be
> Signs to know and words to frame,
> And to spell sweet Jesu's Name.
>
> Then, dear Master, will I look,
> Day and night in that fair book,
> Where the tales of saints are told,
> With their pictures, all in gold.
>
> Teach me, Father John, to say,
> Vesper-verse and matin-lay :
> So when I to God shall plead,
> Christ his Cross shall be my speed.[1]

The whole impression is one of artless simplicity, as naïve in its way as that of Herrick's " Litany," yet we have only to listen to the cadence of the first and last verses to realise that the whole poem is composed with minute attention to detail.

Hawker had as true an ear, and as sweet a note as Tennyson, but because his compass was small, and so attracted but few listeners, he flung his power of song away through neglect. When he ceased to write poetry in 1846, he hid his talent in the earth, and though after some years he dug it up and polished it again, he could never make it the thing of beauty it was at first, for specks of rust still clung to it. It was very much tarnished when he wrote " Baal-Zephon." There is art

[1] " Cornish Ballads," p. 136.

in the first verse of " The Legend of St. Thekla," but
it forces itself on the reader's attention as in the early
poems.

> Sweet is the shrinking image of the rose
>   When her first blush is o'er the mossy ground :
> Her brow is bent where many a blossom grows :
>   She gazes on the flowers that shine around,
> Till with the breath of spring her spirit glows,
>   And her young branch with lifted leaves is crowned.
> Then must her eyes be raised from that low sod,
> She bares her breast to heaven and yields her hues to God.[1]

" Miriam : Star of the Sea," wonderful piece of music
as it is, lacks the purity of sound in the 1840 poems.
Its most beautiful verse is followed by one where sincerity struggles in the trappings of artifice.

> Wave after wave rolls on in ceaseless billow ;
>   Age cannot tame th'unconquerable tide !
> Yon visible surge is but the stately pillow
>   Where the wild storms of ancient waters died.

> Thou Star of Peace ! glory and gladness blending,
>   Here as we lowly kneel, look love on high ;
> Hail, blessed orb ! alive with light descending,
>   A lamp to lead us to our native sky.[2]

When we look at " The Quest of the Sangraal," we
see there, too, signs of decadence. He uses the devices of
alliteration and assonance, partly to give the mediæval
atmosphere, and partly because he cannot help doing
so. Some of the lines are merely ingenious exercises.
What point is there in the alliteration of the following,

> The vassal of the Vase, at Avalon.[3]

or

> The myth and meaning of this marvellous bowl ? [4]

---

[1] " Cornish Ballads," p. 152.
[2] *Ibid.*, p. 155.
[3] *Ibid.*, p. 175.
[4] *Ibid.*, p. 177.

What part does it play but that of unnecessary decoration in the following ?

> Thus came that type and token of our kind,
> The realm and region of the set of sun,
>   The wide, wide West.[1]

It is not as if he was bound by an inexorable pattern of line as were the Anglo-Saxon poets. Though with something of their attitude of mind towards his art, he cannot forego all that the centuries have given in flexibility and subtlety of rhythm and metre, and his " hunting the letter " is too often merely conceit. He scorns it in the words—some of the finest in the poem —which come straight from his heart.

> Ah me ! a gloom falls heavy on my soul—
> The birds that sung to me in youth are dead ;
> I think, in dreaming vigils of the night,
> It may be God is angry with my land,
> Too much athirst for fame, too fond of blood ;
> And all for earth, for shadows, and the dream
> To glean an echo from the winds of song ! [2]

Yet even in the " Sangraal," Hawker's use of alliteration justifies itself. Even though it is becoming the plaything of his old age, he has not quite lost control of it. The terror expressed by the lines on Hell[3] is intensified, and an added dignity given to the words on the Crucifixion, by the contrasts in sound.

> Slowly He died, a world in every pang,
> Until the hard centurion's cruel spear
> Smote His high heart, and from that severed side
> Rush'd the red stream that quencht the wrath of Heaven.[4]

Hawker's use of alliteration and assonance has been treated at length not on account of its poetic value, but because it is part of his idiosyncrasy as a poet. It is

---

[1] " Cornish Ballads," p. 179.
[2] *Ibid.*, p. 186.
[3] *Ibid.*, p. 179.
[4] *Ibid.*, p. 174.

interesting too, that he should make it one of the chief
ornaments of his verse at the same time that Tennyson was developing its music. It is most unlikely that
Hawker owed anything to Tennyson ; he knew
Spenser, Shakespeare and Milton well, but probably
was not acquainted with Tennyson's writings until
after 1840, and by that time his own art was at its
best. But in Hawker's hands the use of alliteration and
assonance becomes a double-edged weapon far more
harmful than it ever was to Tennyson. In Hawker's
poetry they lose the charm of novelty, and their
music palls, for his ear became dulled and his taste
vitiated. As he grew older, he used these devices without restraining them by rhythm, and they soon got out
of hand. We must judge him by his best, and though
there is little originality or subtlety, we cannot deny
him command of his instrument. Rhythm and poetical
devices go hand in hand to produce the desired effect
of loathing in the verse on Judas Iscariot.

> Hail ! Master mine ! so did the viper hiss,
>   When with false fang and stealthy crawl he came
> And scorched Messiah's cheek with that vile kiss
>   He deemed would sojourn there—a brand of shame.[1]

Hawker's use of ornament overloads his verse because he is not a subtle metrist. Skill in prosody is the
result of deliberate training on the part of a poet, and
Hawker paid no attention to the development of his
metrical art. It is sufficient, but nothing more. A poem
never fails because its technique is poor, but neither
does Hawker produce anything new or original. Yet
though one of Hawker's first critics remarked of his
verse, " The lines are always musical, sweet and scan-
able,"[2] there is nothing in them of the tameness that
such a description would suggest. There is certainly
nothing startling about them, for Hawker was no in-
novator in metre, but an artist with a solid literary

[1] " Cornish Ballads," p. 96.
[2] F. G. Lee, " Memorials," p. 87.

education, and he is interesting not for his discovery of new forms and movements, but for the use he makes of stock ones. He has a great variety of musical tunes running through his head, for from his boyhood he had loved those writings where the music of the English tongue is finest, and his retentive memory was a hindrance rather than a help in his own writing. Indeed sometimes even the words of the original force themselves into his verse. We hear the cadences of the Authorised Version in the second verse of " The Lost Ship "—" They went down to thy waves with joyous pride ; "[1] we hear an echo of Scott in the words, " Closing day gilds with soft light their locks of grey,"[2] and of Milton in the words of " The Sangraal," " For evil days came on, and evil men."[3]

But though we may be quite certain of the source of Hawker's music, he generally makes it his own. The ballad of " Sir Beville—The Gate-Song of Stowe " bears no resemblance to the poem on which we know it was formed—Moore's " She is far from the land where her young hero sleeps." One verse may be quoted to show his individual touch.

Ride ! ride ! with red spur, there is death in delay,
  'Tis a race for dear life with the devil ;
If dark Cromwell prevail, and the King must give way,
  This earth is no place for Sir Beville.[4]

Nearly all Hawker's poems, even though written in hackneyed measure, are lifted out of the commonplace by some little personal touch of genius. It may be in variation of rhythm from verse to verse, as in " Modryb Marya," or in his choice of different types and arrangements of the same stanza to fit the various movements of poems, or simply in his use of poetical devices. Indeed, his apparent lack of originality in verse itself marks him a true poet, for the simplest and

1 " Cornish Ballads," p. 97.
2 *Ibid.*, p. 95.
3 *Ibid.*, p. 175.
4 *Ibid.*, p. 167.

the oldest metres were the ones best suited for themes such as his, and those which had come down from the earliest times of English song especially fitting for a poet so typically English as Hawker to use.

In his choice of verse-forms Hawker is led by two desires. He loves the " jingling sound of like endings," and he loves a sweeping rhythm. So poem after poem is written in couplets ; the lines may have three, four or five beats, and be arranged in stanzas of varying length, but they are made to move in as orderly and restrained a fashion as when poets were still in thrall to the couplet. It would be difficult to find a more un-enterprising verse than the first one of " Ephphatha."

> High matins now in bower and hall !
> It is the Baptist's festival :
> What showers of gold the sunbeams rain,
> Through the tall window's purple pane !
> What rich hues on the pavement lie,
> A molten rainbow from the sky ! [1]

And yet the whole poem gives a feeling of satisfaction through the perfect welding of thought and form and style. The finest poem of the 1832 volume, " The Silent Tower of Bottreaux," which Professor Saintsbury considers " very much more of a diploma piece "[2] than the others, is written in couplets, but the touch of genius is on it in the variation from a four-beat to a three-beat movement in the refrain. The verse of " Words by the Waters," three pentameter lines followed by an Alexandrine, and rhymed in couplets, is given individuality by its long-drawn concluding line.

As was only natural, Hawker's other best-loved metre was the ballad measure and its many variations. But his love of rhyme made him scorn the easy task of writing true ballad measure with its unrhymed first and third lines, and all Hawker's are fully equipped with rhyme. He has a very sure hand in all his varia-

---

[1] " Cornish Ballads," p. 73.
[2] Camb. Hist. of Eng. Lit., vol. XII., p. 134.

tions of this measure, and though he seldom uses one,
is especially skilful in managing a refrain. We see art
in his delicacy of touch in dealing with subjects of
very different emotional value. Sheer mischievous fun
breathes through the verse of " A Cornish Folk Song."

> Now of all the birds that keep the tree,
>   Which is the wittiest fowl ?
> Oh, the Cuckoo—the Cuckoo's the one !—for he
>   Is wiser than the owl ! [1]

Very different is the insight into the grim meaning of
Prussian militarism which underlies the superficial
jollity of the form of " The Carol of the Pruss."

> " Up ! " said the King, " load, fire and slay !
>   'Tis a kindly signal given :
> However happy on earth be they,
>   They'll be happier in heaven.
> Tell them, as soon as their souls are free,
> They'll sing like birds on a Christmas tree ! " [2]

All Hawker's powers as a metrist are epitomised in a
comparison between this poem and another of very
different meaning where he uses the same stanza. He
has the gift of producing atmosphere, of attaining the
right emotional effect. The contrast is made more
striking by the similarity of language, for the third
verse of " Modryb Marya "—a poem on the holly—
runs,

> 'Tis a bush that the birds will never leave :
>   They sing in it all day long ;
> But sweetest of all upon Christmas Eve,
>   Is to hear the robin's song.
> 'Tis the merriest sound upon earth and sea ;
> For it comes from our own Aunt Mary's tree.[3]

We come by gradual stages through the serious note
struck in the varying words of the refrain in " The

[1] " Cornish Ballads," p. 203.
[2] Ibid., p. 211.
[3] Ibid., p. 46.

Silent Tower of Bottreaux " to the solemnity of "King Arthur's Waes-hael."

> Waes-hael! in shadowy scene,
>   Lo! Christmas children we;
> Drink-hael! behold we lean
>   At a fair Mother's knee;
> To dream, that thus her bosom smiled,
> And learn the lip of Bethlehem's Child.[1]

The use made by Hawker of other rhymed stanzas reveals the same power of wedding thought and music. He learnt from Gray the fitness of " elegiac stanza " for slow-moving meditative verse, and used it to good purpose in " The Token-Stream of Tonacombe," a poem interesting as an illustration of a time when " second thoughts were best," for he had earlier attempted to write on the same subject in heroic couplets. Two interesting variations of it are seen in the poems, " Miriam : Star of the Sea " and " Aishah Schechinah." The difference between their music shows the height of Hawker's art.

> I am the Sea, that treacherous, swells for ever,
> And ebbs and flows with one unceasing stream !
> Thou art the Star, whose radiance faileth never,
> Calm o'er the billows waves its faithful beam ! [2]

Very different is the movement of the other poem on the Virgin, for its meaning is to inspire awe rather than to sing of love.

> Round her, too pure to mingle with the day,
>   Light, that was life, abode ;
> Folded within her fibres meekly lay
>   The link of boundless God.[3]

Hawker is more successful in short stanzas than in elaborate ones. He learns Spenserian Stanza from Byron and uses it quite skilfully in " Minster Church,"

---

[1] " Cornish Ballads," p. 166.
[3] *Ibid.*, p. 155.
[2] *Ibid.*, p. 161.

where he is able to give a succession of pictures, but when many years later he attempts to write narrative poems in eight-lined stanzas, the effect is not so pleasing. He has not at his command the richness of imagery or the fecundity of thought which a long stanza must have, if it is not to drag out its length " like a wounded snake." In his prime he knew this himself, and instead of using Spenserian stanza, applied its most characteristic feature to other forms of verse. One of his favourite devices is to round off a series of pentameter lines with one containing an extra foot.

> Why dost thou wait and watch the gloomy shore,
> Where the rocks darken and the surges roar,—
> While down the steep the foamy cataract raves,
> And rolls dissolved amid the wilderness of waves ? [1]

Here the long sweeping rhythm adds to the beauty of the verse, but it is harder to justify its existence at the end of a sonnet. And though Hawker wrote several so-called sonnets, we cannot include that form among his master-pieces. The only one with a recognised rhyme-plan, (" Pater Vester Pascit Illa "), ends with an Alexandrine, and in all the others Hawker's love of closely linked rhymes made him adopt an original plan *a b b a c c a d d*, often carried on for more than fourteen lines. And then the poems are no longer sonnets, but ingeniously-linked sets of couplets. Hawker's mind was too diffuse and rambling to be able to use the beautiful compactness of the sonnet to the highest advantage.

Hawker prided himself on his skill in workmanship. Two letters sent to " Notes and Queries " in 1834 show him correcting correspondents who had misquoted his verses, for he " cannot receive praise for false metre and erroneous grammar."[2] Few poets have been more precise than he, and few have loved rhyme more. He writes to Dr. F. G. Lee on the subject of his Newdi-

---

[1] " Cornish Ballads," p. 125.
[2] " Notes and Queries," vol. IX., 1st Series, p. 231. *V.* also p. 135.

gate Prize Poem," The Martyrs of Vienne and Lyons,"
" Why in rhymeless verses ? You, too, who can rule
the sound so well. It may be that I rather eschew the
metre from horror at the false fame of that double-
dyed thief of other men's brains—John Milton, the
Puritan."[1] No doubt this fantastic reason was not the
true one, but it is surely of more than ordinary significance when such a poet drops the device of rhyme.
Hawker writes three poems in unrhymed lines. In
each he lays bare his deepest thoughts, each appears a
fragment, yet is complete in itself, and each represents
a period of his life. In his youth he writes " A Rapture
on the Cornish Hills ; " in late middle age, " The Quest
of the Sangraal ; " and in old age, " $\dot{\epsilon}\nu$ $\dot{a}\rho\chi\eta$."

In these poems Hawker is the mystic rather than
the conscious artist ; for him blank verse is the language of inspiration in the same way that it was for
Blake. His verse is closer to established forms than
Blake's, but it is quite as individual. Hawker's other
metres are old ; his blank verse is his own. Even the
great teachers of his youth, Shakespeare and Milton,
have helped him but little in its development. We hear
it first, irregular yet musical, in " A Rapture."

> I stood at the foot of Rocky Carradon—
> The massive monuments of a vast religion,
> Piled by the strength of unknown hands, were there.
> The everlasting hills, around, afar,
> Uplifted their huge fronts, the natural altars
> Reared by the Earth to the surrounding God.[2]

There is more art in the " Sangraal," but the measure
has even less freedom. While Tennyson was giving to
blank verse a greater flexibility of rhythm and a
music more subtle than it had ever had, Hawker
moulded it with a rugged strength, which he could
gain only by taking from it all its grace, its polish—in
short, its sophistication—and making it almost as un-
couth as it had been in its earliest days. As far as the

---

[1] " Life and Letters," p. 232.
[2] " Cornish Ballads," p. 38.

movement of the verse is concerned, some of the passages might have been written before Shakespeare. How much " cribbed, cabin'd and confined " it is we may see from the lines spoken by Arthur.

> Ay ! all beside can win companionship :
> The churl may clip his mate beneath the thatch,
> While his brown urchins nestle at his knees :
> The soldier give and grasp a mutual palm,
> Knit to his flesh in sinewy bonds of war :
> The knight may seek at eve his castle-gate,
> Mount the old stair, and lift the accustomed latch,
> To find, for throbbing brow and weary limb,
> That paradise of pillows, one true breast :
> But he, the lofty ruler of the land,
> Like yonder Tor, first greeted by the dawn,
> And wooed the latest by the lingering day,
> With happy homes and hearths beneath his breast,
> Must soar and gleam in solitary snow.
> The lonely one is, evermore, the King.[1]

It is this very restriction of the power of the metre which gives the verse of the " Sangraal " its individuality. It has an antique flavour which well suits a poem on the mediæval, and its frequent alliteration reminds us of those early alliterative romances on Arthur and his knights. Only its more finished harmony stamps it as the product of a less spontaneous age, the work of a man who was born late enough to choose his metre and his ornaments from poetry through the centuries. By blending the forms of a new measure, for such was blank verse in the fifteenth century, and the ornaments of a dying tradition, for by that time the alliterative line had done its best work, Hawker evolved a measure which carried with it something of the spirit of the Middle Ages. It is this which makes the verse of the " Sangraal " original, and gives it the " vigour and independence "[2] for which Professor Saintsbury praises it. It owes nothing to poetry of its own time. No wonder Hawker called the

[1] " Cornish Ballads," p. 185.
[2] Camb. Hist. of Eng. Lit., vol. XII., p. 134.

L

reviewer who suggested that he had imitated Tennyson, " an utter donkey," and continued, " If he means that I write in the same metre as Tennyson no one but an idiot would call that imitation any more than Milton could be called a copyist, because he wrote his ' Paradise Lost ' in the common metre of his own day and of those who went before him."[1] Though not as grand a poetic vehicle as the blank verse of the great poets, Hawker's has a virility which is sometimes lacking in more finished verse, and a felicity of phrase which lifts it far above the commonplace. We must not look for elaborate similes, wide landscapes, or rolling harmonies. Hawker's verse is like his own wild seacoast, rugged but strong, and power as free and boundless as that of the wind and the sea pulses through it. Like only great poetry it appeals to the emotions as well as to the intellect, and its sincerity makes it grand.

> Forth gleamed the east, and yet it was not day !
> A white and glowing horse outrode the dawn ;
> A youthful rider ruled the bounding rein,
> And he, in semblance of Sir Galahad shone :
> A vase he held on high ; one molten gem,
> Like massive ruby or the chrysolite :
> Thence gushed the light in flakes ; and flowing, fell
> As though the pavement of the sky brake up,
> And stars were shed to sojourn on the hills,
> From grey Morwenna's stone to Michael's tor,
> Until the rocky land was like a heaven.[2]

The oft-quoted concluding lines show his music in a different key.

> He ceased ; and all around was dreamy night :
> There stood Dundagel, throned ; and the great sea
> Lay, a strong vassal at his master's gate,
> And, like a drunken giant, sobb'd in sleep ! [3]

" The Quest of the Sangraal " is the only poem of Hawker's where it is possible to do justice to him in

[1] " Life and Letters," p. 457.
[2] " Cornish Ballads," p. 188.
[3] *Ibid.*, p. 190.

extracts. In this, matter and style make it great in spite of a defect in form, but in his shorter poems Hawker's greatness lies in his perfect expression of emotion and thought in poetic form and music. They are few in number, for, as we have already seen, Hawker's poetic genius was stifled, and his energy diverted into other channels, but they show the quality of his inspiration. He is a master in lyric of a subdued tone. The pure lyrical quality which was his birthright was nearly always held back ; like the bird in his own crest, the falcon,[1] it was tamed by a stronger power. The singer was controlled by the mystic. But that Hawker could write pure lyric is shown by the quality of the verses, " Dangerous Eyes," which were not written until he was over sixty.

> The eyes that melt, the eyes that burn,
> The lips that make a lover yearn,
> These flashed on my bewildered sight,
> Like meteors of the northern night.
>
> Then said I in my wild amaze,
> " What stars be they that greet my gaze ?
> Where shall my shivering rudder turn ?—
> To eyes that melt, or eyes that burn ? "
>
> Ah ! safer far the darkling sea,
> Than where such perilous signals be ;
> To rock and storm, and whirlwind turn
> From eyes that melt and eyes that burn." [2]

Intense as Hawker's feelings were, they were seldom allowed to appear as nakedly as this. He would not let himself sing : his mission was to teach, and instruction is ever a leaden weight to keep poetry fluttering near the earth. Hawker's power as an artist can only be measured by his success in raising such material " on the viewless wings of poesy," for he expresses himself fully only when his mystical and artistic powers are perfectly wedded. Only in his poetry

---

[1] *V.* " Life and Letters," p. 577.
[2] " Cornish Ballads," p. 193.

L 2

does he touch greatness, and even in that he has many
limitations. Putting aside the question of bulk, and
considering the worth of his actual achievement, we
are forced to admit some serious short-comings. He is
a man of one idea, the linking of religion and life, and,
though that idea is the greatest a poet may have, he
approaches it along a narrow road. He has, therefore,
but a restricted range of appeal. He is unoriginal in
form, and his verse, though musical, is often monotonous, and sometimes marred by idiosyncrasy : yet,
in spite of all, there is something in his poetry which
makes the reading of it a delight. It breathes the
spirit of the man, and is original because Hawker had
a rich and varied personality. It is as fascinating as its
author. In his verse, as in his character, spiritual vision
goes hand in hand with deep human sympathies, and
an abiding joy in the beauty of the natural world, and
in the expression of this he is unique. For Hawker is
the poet of the Catholic faith, and his work must be
judged with that of other sacred poets, rather than
with that of Wordsworth and Shelley, so infinitely
greater than he in spiritual perception and in teaching
its application to life. His province is one which they
left untouched, the debatable ground of religion
bounded by institution and form ; and so he is a fellow-
worker in another sphere of action rather than a potential rival. It is only in comparison with other
writers of sacred verse that his genius shines out.

Religious poetry falls inevitably into two classes.
In the one the writer's personality bursts its fetters of
reserve, and sings of his vision out of the fullness of
passion in his heart ; in the other the poet looks on
himself as the instrument of God, and his individuality
is held back, so that only his purpose appears. The
study of Hawker's life has shown to which he belongs,
and we cannot compare him with writers of the first
type. He is not on the same plane with the seventeenth
century religious poets—the children of an introspec-
tive and somewhat self-conscious age. Crashaw, carried

away by the passion of his faith, sings spontaneously
of very love and joy, Herbert in quieter mood describes the ardour of his search for the peace of God.
Vaughan tries to express for his own relief the lessons
which the Church and nature hold for him, Traherne
rejoices in his state of felicity, More analyses the workings of his soul. The intimacy of their poetry gives it
at times a depth of spiritual intensity, a power of
lyrical expression, which Hawker never touches. But
the seventeenth century was an age of song, Hawker's
an age of instruction ; and a comparison of his poetry
with that of other nineteenth century religious verse
brings out its value.

The Oxford Movement was heralded and accom-
panied by sacred verse. None of it soared very high,
for the writers were either men whom religion had
made poets, or poets who put the Church before their
art. Newman, the truest artist of them all, said that
poetry was " the refuge of those who have not the
Catholic Church to flee to and repose upon,"[1] and in
consequence ranks as a poet only by reason of a few
hymns and " The Dream of Gerontius." All the others
owed much to Wordsworth in inspiration and form,
and his remarks on two of them are not without interest. Wordsworth's estimate of Keble's most important contribution to poetry, " The Christian Year,"
was that " it was so good that if it were his he would
rewrite it,"[2] and he told Faber that when he took the
Church as his profession England lost a poet.[3]

Hawker comes into his own when placed beside
these. He has a vitality which is lacking in them, for
there is nothing second-hand in his inspiration. Keble's
poetry with all its sincerity, its faith, its gentle beauty,
is monotone, that of Isaac Williams a " pale companion." They are presenting religious ideas in poetic
form ; Hawker is singing of reality. Their verse is like

---

[1] Hugh Walker, " Literature of the Victorian Era," p. 340.
[2] Camb. Hist. of Eng. Lit., vol. XIII., p. 168.
[3] *Ibid.*, p. 171.

a limpid stream, Hawker's a sparkling mountain torrent. Hawker has done just what Keble could not do, for, according to Professor Hugh Walker, " The elements of Keble's verse lie side by side, mingled, but not fused. We see the nature-poet in one stanza, the religious poet in the next. He lacks the art to conceal art, or better the glow of feeling which effects the concealment unconsciously."[1] The power to resolve all the elements of thought into a perfect whole is one of Hawker's most characteristic qualities, and marks him a poet indeed. The unity in his own imagination makes his thoughts poetry. Though he belongs to the second class of poets, his individuality is so strong that it is reflected through the objective poems, and they are great because the man himself was great. The poems in which his genius speaks are ones which " the world will not willingly let die," as he himself echoed Milton.

In his small and limited way, with his view bounded by Morwenstow instead of the world, he has a quality in which no poet surpasses him. It is the power of seeing the spirit in all things, and of stating his vision in such clear and simple words that the most ignorant may carry something away. " I seek to be understood by the lowest capacity,"[2] we find jotted in the notes, and again, " A ready and boundless grasp of the simplest and truest words is the real triumph."[3] He has achieved his ambition. No other modern poet has brought the Church so close to the lives of the people as Hawker has done, and he has succeeded in his aim by applying its teaching to things within their ken, local legends, local sights, local events. And though the subjects are trivial, by his art Hawker has lifted them out of the ordinary, and has made the particular of universal import. His poems are parables ; they teach " that humbler things may

[1] " Literature of the Victorian Era," p. 263.
[2] Unpublished.
[3] Unpublished.

fondly dream of mysteries divine."[1] Some are deep,
some simple, but they appeal not only to the unletter-
ed Cornish peasants for whom they were written, but
by reason of his genius to any who love poetry. In his
work of offering spiritual truth in various forms to
suit different types of minds, he has gained a wideness
of appeal which only the great poets surpass. " A
Christ-Cross Rhyme " is a child's poem, yet the most
critical can find pleasure in the beauty of its simplicity.
On the other hand, " Aishah Schechinah " expresses
the philosophy of the Incarnation in terms of flesh and
blood.

> A shape like folded light, embodied air,
>   Yet wreath'd with flesh, and warm ;
> All that of heaven is feminine and fair,
>   Moulded in visible form.
>
> She stood, the Lady Schechinah of earth,
>   A chancel for the sky ;
> Where woke, to breath and beauty, God's own birth
>   For men to see him by.
>
> Round her, too pure to mingle with the day,
>   Light, that was life, abode ;
> Folded within her fibres meekly lay
>   The link of boundless God.[2]

And there are many poems between these two ex-
tremes. There are poems like "The Bells of Bottreaux,"
or " The Quest of the Sangraal," for those to whom
stories appeal, the first with an obvious meaning, the
second with a hidden one beneath. There is " Morwennae Statio," which may be read as a descriptive poem,
or " Ephphatha " which, though its subject is the
Eucharist, holds no philosophy, but shows again the
simplicity of art. His simple but artistic presentation
of the spiritual is the ground of Hawker's claim to be
recognised as a true poet. It is the mark of all his
finest poems, but none shows it more perfectly than a

---

[1] " Cornish Ballads," p. 108.
[2] *Ibid.*, p. 161.

short poem, " addressed to the late Arthur Mills, Esq.,
M.P. on the completion of his house, ' Efford Down,'
at Bude." Even such a prosaic idea as that of a new
Victorian house may be given a significance outside
the limits of Time and Space.

> A fair and stately scene of roof and walls,
>   Touched by the ruddy sunsets of the West ;
> Where, meek and molten, eve's soft radiance falls
>   Like golden feathers in the ringdove's nest.
>
> Yonder the bounding sea, that couch of God !
>   A wavy wilderness of sand between,
> Such pavement, in the Syrian deserts, trod
>   Bright forms, in girded albs, of heavenly mien.
>
> Such saw the patriarch in his noon-day tent :
>   Three severed shapes that glided in the sun,
> Till lo ! they cling, and interfused and blent
>   A lovely semblance gleams—the Three in One !
>
> Be such the scenery of this peaceful ground—
>   This leafy tent amid the wilderness :
> Fair skies above, the breath of Angels round,
>   And God the Trinity to beam and bless ![1]

It is his intense realisation that " the very ground
with speech is fraught, the air is eloquent of God,"[2]
which will make Hawker's poems live.

Yet this is not enough to mark him off from other
poets. There is, however, an element in his poetry
which does this, and we come back to the characteristic quality of his spirit. And what is more elusive,
more difficult to describe than spirit ? It is something
to be felt, not to be analysed, and one is loth to touch
it, lest words deal as harshly with it as the clumsy
fingers which crush a butterfly's wing. Hawker's poetry
has few " purple patches ; " it is difficult to extract
beauties of thought or expression, for the effect is
made by the whole poem, but over all there is a

[1] " Cornish Ballads," p. 202.
[2] *Ibid.*, p. 49.

glamour by right of which it belongs to the land of "faerie." It enthralls as some poems of greater worth can never do, for Hawker is the Wizard of the South, though he has had as yet few readers on whom to lay his charm. "Queen Guennivar's Round" is but a single wave of his wand.

> Naiad for Grecian waters!
>   Nymph for the fountain-side!
> But old Cornwall's bounding daughters
>   For grey Dundagel's tide.
>
> The wild wind proudly gathers
>   Round the ladies of the land;
> And the blue wave of their fathers
>   Is joyful where they stand.
>
> Naiad for Grecian waters!
>   Nymph for the fountain-side!
> But old Cornwall's bounding daughters
>   For grey Dundagel's tide.
>
> Yes! when memory rejoices
>   In her long beloved theme,
> Fair forms and thrilling voices
>   Will mingle with my dream.
>
> Naiad for Grecian waters!
>   Nymph for the fountain-side!
> But old Cornwall's bounding daughters
>   For grey Dundagel's tide.[1]

Hawker's genius is a Cornish one, and though he is greater than a merely local poet, he is original because the fervour of the Celt breathes through all he writes. His spiritual vision is inseparable from his love of the wild Cornish coast, its angry sea, its frowning headlands, its rocky moors; and the reflection of its rugged beauty in sun and shadow through his own life and character is his heritage. Though he is much more than the "Poet of Cornwall," we cannot refuse to grant the desire expressed in the dedication to one of his early

[1] "Cornish Ballads," p. 102.

volumes, for he owes much to his race and the land of his birth.

> Hills of old Cornwall ! in your antique fame
> Oh ! that a voice unborn might blend my future name ![1]

Finally we must consider Hawker's place in the literary history of his time. It is interesting to note the positions assigned to him by writers on the literature of the period in which he lived and wrote. They find him a problem : he wrote too little to be worthy of much notice, and yet he is as detached as only a great poet has the right to be. Professor Hugh Walker solves the difficulty by dissecting his work, and treats of him first as a ballad-writer,[2] and then as a Catholic poet, this latter solely on account of " The Quest of the Sangraal."[3] Had he included the other religious poems in his survey, he would have seen the unity underlying all Hawker's poetry, and the injustice done to him if it is arbitrarily divided into secular and religious. As a writer of historical ballad he is imitative and mediocre ; as a poet who in the nineteenth century caught the meaning of the mediæval acceptance of religion, and tried to express it with the simplicity, the sincerity and the beauty which breathed through the mediæval ballad of either type, he stands alone.

Yet Professor Hugh Walker in his treatment of Hawker shows a far deeper understanding of the man and his work than Professor Saintsbury. The latter forces him into a crowd of " lesser poets," who flourished, roughly, from 1790—1837,[4] among whom he certainly does appear a lost sheep. We feel that he is placed there solely from a prosodic view of his poetry, and that the forms of his verse have taken undue precedence of its spirit. Such an attitude cannot fail to be unjust to his genius. For, as a metrist, he was indeed a Janus " of the backward face only,"[5] but we must

---

[1] " Cornish Ballads," p. xxv.
[2] " Literature of the Victorian Era." p. 330.
[3] *Ibid.*, p. 342.
[4] Camb. Hist. of Eng. Lit., vol. XII., ch. v.
[5] *Ibid.*, p. 139.

take into account his own ordering of his career. He never intended to make the writing of poetry his chief business in life ; he never attempted to develop his art ; and the teachers of his youth remained those of his manhood. A comparison of Hawker's life with Tennyson's brings his position into relief. His six years' seniority was just enough to prevent his gaining any knowledge of Keats or Shelley[1] before burying himself in Cornwall, hence his dependence on the older group of poets, and during the ten years in which Tennyson was developing and polishing his craft, Hawker's energies were set on Christianizing " a population previously little better than savages." Surely the spirit is worth more than the form. Moreover, viewed in this way, Hawker is neither a poet of the transition period, nor a solitary vagrant. And as Professor Saintsbury seems to expect some demur to be made to his estimate of Hawker, one would like to suggest that the poet would be more at home with some of the next group of lesser poets, with Keble, Newman, Isaac Williams, Faber and Neale ; and that, considering that the poetry of each of these has received double notice,[2] half a paragraph is but scant measure for one who was as true a poet as any of them.

There are several reasons for placing him with the sacred, or Catholic, poets. The first is the relatively unimportant one of chronology. His production, feeble and intermittent as it was, extended over fifty years of the nineteenth century, from 1821 to 1874, and his finest poems were not written until after 1837. He was not of the same generation as Heber, the last of the earlier group, whose poems were published posthumously in 1827, but the publication of Hawker's poems marches side by side with that of various writings of the Tractarians. Keble issued " The Christian Year " in 1827. Hawker published volumes of poems in 1832 and 1836. " Lyra Apostolica " appeared

---

[1] v. " Literature of the Victorian Era," p. 293.
[2] Camb. Hist. of Eng. Lit., vol. XII., ch. xii., and vol. XIII., ch. v.

in the same year. Isaac Williams, Faber and Neale issued volumes of poems and hymns at intervals from 1838 to 1860, and Newman's "Dream of Gerontius" appeared in 1866. Hawker's last poem was written in 1874.

But a mere list of dates is of little value, unless they are the signposts which point to movements in the world of thought or of action. In this case they are full of significance. They mean that Hawker and the leaders of the Oxford Movement have something in common. The forces which brought about the Oxford Movement—Scott and his imaginative presentation of the past, the desire for mere beauty than could be found in the present, and the conviction that truth was inseparably linked with that beauty—these moulded Hawker's life ; and though he had no connection with it, he was with the Tractarians in spirit. His field of action was Morwenstow, while theirs was England, but his poetry was the expression of their ideal. Hawker was well-fitted to be the poet-spokesman of a movement " with a religion which was fervent and reforming in essentials with a due reverence for existing authorities and habits and traditions, but it was not narrow or cloistered, it was a religion which did not reject, but aspired to embody in itself any form of art and literature, poetry, philosophy and even science which could be pressed into the service of Christianity."[1] He left his task unfinished, but that should not prevent our seeing his place in the nineteenth century.

The third reason is of less weight. But there can be no doubt that the Tractarians themselves influenced Hawker a little. " The Christian Year " was published before he left Oxford, and in later years he refers to remarks made to him by Keble. Cut off from association with other literary men, he never quite lost touch with Oxford, and he followed the movement of thought there as closely as he could. He watched with interest

[1] Letters of Lord Blachford, p. 15.   Quoted in Camb. Hist. of Eng., vol. XII., p. 277.

the career of Newman, a man with whom he had much in common, and the vagaries of J. B. Morris[1] were paralleled in his own thought. Hawker belongs to the Victorian age. His poetry would not have been what it is, had he lived at any other time, and yet apart from topical poems it bears no marks to date it. It reflects nothing of the intellectual conflicts of the time, nothing of the march of progress, nothing of the fear of facing the truth, of the myopic selfishness[2] which we associate with the middle years of last century. The poet's intense conviction of the eternal reality of spirit has lifted it out of its own time, and made it as detached in its way as Blake's is from the age of rationalism in which he lived. There is an ageless quality in Hawker's finest poems, and like Blake he stands alone ; with but slight literary heritage and no descendants. His isolation is not due to weakness, but to strength : " the lonely one is, evermore, the King."

[1] D.N.B. J. B. Morris. " Eccentric in appearance and manner, he was brimful of genuine and multifarious learning, but so credulous that he seriously believed in the existence of the Phoenix."

[2] *Cf*. Carlyle's " A dim horn-eyed owl-population, intent only on the catching of mice." (Latter-day Pamphlets, 1850, p. 72), repeated twenty years later by Ruskin in " Fors Clavigera."

CONCLUSION.

"IF I print anything in prose or verse, no one cares even to read it. No one notices the thoughts or language — neither the mower nor he that gathereth the sheaves."[1] No longer need we be haunted by the plaintive cry of the unappreciated poet and mystic, but as our task draws to an end, we may well pause to consider if his claim to a hearing has been justified. Has the labour of reaping been repaid by fruitful sheaves ? And the answer to such a question must needs be a personal one, for the saying that " One man's meat is another man's poison " is true also of mental and spiritual food. Hawker never opened his heart to those whom he felt unsympathetic, but those who were willing to listen found him no niggard of his powers.

So it will be with his poetry. He will never be a popular poet, but the fact that his work is " caviare to the general " does not detract from its value. It is but an injustice to Hawker to attempt to win for him select coteries of readers by calling him " The Poet of Cornwall," and " one of our greater religious poets." The result is a foregone conclusion ; the contents may be known by the label, no need to taste for oneself. Hawker is pushed further and further back on the shelf. And yet both labels are true. He *is* the Poet of Cornwall, but not in the limited way in which his neighbour, Barnes, was the poet of Dorset, but rather as Wordsworth was the poet of the Lakes, inspired, sustained by the grandeur of nature, and reaching upward from it towards the eternal verities. He *is* " one

[1] " Life and Letters," p. 277.

of our greater religious poets," but he is great because
as a poet he had his own original contribution to offer
to English religious verse, and his appeal is widened to
all lovers of poetry, whatever their views on theology.
He is closer to Francis Thompson than to Isaac Watts.
He sings of man's apprehension of the spiritual rather
than of moral laws, of faith, hope and love rather than
of works. In short he is a mystic, not a moralist.

In that fact lies his greatness. He belongs to no class
but that of the mystics, and of that every member is
closely akin to his fellow, and yet unique. Each has the
same story to tell, though in varying degrees of lucid-
ity, but each has his method of delivery affected in
some measure by the age in which he lived. The Victorian age was a hard time for sensitive spirits, and
Hawker, in spite of his apparent forcefulness of character, had a "quivering soul." Probably for him it would
have taken less moral courage to join the Roman
Catholic Church and give up his independence of
thought than he needed to remain outside it, wrestling
with doubt. To him, as to Newman, it appeared a calm
haven after storm, and it says much for the strength
of his character that he resisted the temptation practically to the end. The unutterable melancholy which
so often darkened Hawker's vision is but another
proof of his courage, for he, like Tennyson, had to en-
dure the trials of the Mystic Way, unsupported by the
feeling of serene joy which is the endowment of most
mystics. Both Tennyson and Hawker were sorely bat-
tered on the journey, and both lost sight of the goal,
the one standing still to comment on features close at
hand, the other retracing his steps to inspect relics of
the past. But in spite of this Hawker went further than
Tennyson; he can never have the word "Victorian"
flung at him as a gibe, and only those who do not look
below the surface will call him mediæval. Hawker's
poems with the setting of an older time have a meaning for every age; Tennyson's, first and foremost, for
his own. While Hawker's Arthurian poem preserves

the mediæval atmosphere, and yet has a modern appeal, Tennyson makes no attempt to keep the one, and fails to attain the other, because he colours his theme with Victorian sentiment, and bows to Victorian convention. Hawker could not find words forceful enough to denounce the age in which he lived, and his clear-eyed perception of its faults makes him essentially modern.

He was far in advance of his own time, and in some of his views ahead of ours. His conception of the Church is an ideal which is still far from being realised, for he saw it as a unity towards which all man's various energies should flow, and in which they should find their highest expression. He tried to bring it into relation with humble life and with progressive thought —to apply its teaching to the labours of Morwenstow peasants, and the researches of scientists. The task which he set himself is the one which confronts all sections of religious thought to-day, for one of the most urgent problems before the modern Church is the cleavage between itself and life. It was no less important in Hawker's time. Keble, with his own clear vision of the·sacredness of life, saw the need of making the Church popular, and the great work ready for a man who would treat the history of the Church as Scott had dealt with Scottish history and legend.[1] It was a work akin to that of Blake—the work of reviving spirit, of making dry bones live, of plucking down hollow beliefs and putting Truth and Beauty in their place. Though Hawker left his work unfinished—partly through a fatal weakness in his own character, and partly through the circumstances of his life—that was his ideal, and he never degraded his gift of poetry by trying to win the Victorian ear. He accuses Tennyson of cutting " anything Churchy " as it " would have been fatal to his future fame in England."[2] He himself has a title to fame only as the poet of the Church.

[1] Camb. Hist. of Eng. Lit., vol. XII., p. 255.
[2] " Life and Letters," p. 415.

For a mystic Hawker is extraordinarily impersonal in his religious poetry. Though living in the nineteenth century, when the power of the Church as a social institution was waning, he was far more controlled by it than many of the mediæval mystics who wrote down their own convictions at a time when the Church exacted implicit obedience from her members. Though the son of that Church of England which has always laid as much stress on the value of personal inspiration as on that of traditional belief, he chose a road till then untrodden, and became the poet of the Catholic Faith more truly than either Crashaw or his follower, Francis Thompson. In an ecstasy of lyrical fervour they sang of its appeal to their own souls ; Hawker, in more restrained verse, set forth its universal power—the true catholicity of its teaching—for young and old, for rich and poor, for learned and ignorant. " One Faith, one Church, one Heaven will join the labourer and his lord."[1] His gift to English poetry was the imaginative presentation of the truths of Christianity, truths founded on Divine revelation but supported by the lessons of nature, and his mission to insist on their reality beyond the limits of Space and Time. In his method he is the follower of Scott and of Byron, in much of his thought the companion of Wordsworth and his predecessor, Vaughan ; in his attitude of mind he is of the seventeenth century, yet in spite of all he owes to men before him, he is original and progressive.

Hawker's message, with its romantic background of the past, was one for his own generation, and has not yet lost its force. The material world still looms large before us : we have not yet reached Wordsworth's conception of science in a state when " it shall be ready to put on as it were a form of flesh and blood," when " the poet will lend his Divine spirit to aid the transformation, and will welcome the Being thus produced as a dear and genuine inmate of the household

---

[1] " Cornish Ballads," p. 131.

M

of man."[1] Wordsworth and Shelley lit a torch which
has not yet given light to us, and though it was but
flickering in Hawker's writings, he is a link in the
chain, and we have not yet completed it. We have not
yet spiritualised physical science, though we have
prophets who bid us be ready for the venture. When
that time comes, will not his vaunt also be fulfilled ?
" Hereafter my verses will be sought after, sold, illustrated, read, aye and extolled to the very echo. The
Ballads will be called by every noble name—and then
will come the ower-true tale ' In his life-time they
could find no printer brave enough to shed his ink in
their behalf and so they died.' "[2]

Yet, true poet as he is in thought and expression,
we cannot consider Hawker a great poet. He gives
nothing to the technique of verse-writing, and though
the quality of his poetry is high, the quantity is meagre. He is interesting rather than great, for, original
though he was, he is yet another of a peculiarly English type of poet. There is a great company of priests
of the Church of England who have become famous
for their literary work as poets or philosophers, and
Hawker is no alien among them. But they fall into
sharply-defined groups, dependent chiefly on the
quality of life in the Church, and owing to a certain
similarity in conditions, those of the seventeenth century approach those of the nineteenth. But for most of
the Victorians the retired life possible even during the
tumult of the Civil War was a thing desired, not granted. Keble, Isaac Williams, Newman, Kingsley had to
enter into the lists ; Hawker alone had seclusion like
that of George Herbert, Henry More, Thomas Traherne or John Norris. And he is interesting because he
shows the idiosyncrasy of the English character repeating itself. Nourished on the same food—the Early
Fathers of the Church—and set in similar retirement,
he touches more than one figure of the seventeenth

---

[1] Dean Inge, " Christian Mysticism," p. 322.
[2] " Life and Letters," p. 384.

century very closely. He has antiquarian interests like Sir Thomas Browne, his mental attitude is that of Henry More, his artistic equipment close to that of George Herbert. He is even nearer to Herbert's disciple, Henry Vaughan. Both are artists and mystics with an intensely devotional spirit, who find the meaning of life revealed in the phenomena of the natural world as well as in the teaching of the Church. To both each wonder of nature is " a lamp to lead some pathway of the Lord,"[1] and Hawker, like Vaughan, loves to meditate above all on the stars, on the movement of water, and on the birds of the air. Though Hawker had probably no knowledge of Vaughan except through Wordsworth, his work stands in relation to Vaughan's in something the same way as Francis Thompson's to Crashaw's. It is the nineteenth century presentation, in a new and original setting, of ideas first expressed by a seventeenth century thinker. For that reason, if for no other, Hawker has been too long ignored by lovers of English poetry.

Yet when all is said we come back to our starting point. Hawker's poetry is worth study because the man himself was great, as his first biographers realised. We have studied him chiefly as mystic and poet, but in doing so have come as close to the danger of giving but one side only of the man as did Mr. Baring-Gould and Dr. Lee. We must remember actions as well as consider thoughts in order to form our mental picture of the whole man, but surely our plan is justified if he who before was contemptuously termed " a little crazy " may be understood and appreciated as a great personality. The absurdities, the extravagances, the little vanities fade into insignificance beside the courage, the self-sacrifice, the devotion of Hawker's life, and his real, though slight and fitful, genius. Cornwall —nay, England, for such is its symbolic meaning in the poem, may well be proud of her son. It is her privilege to bring true his words :

[1] " Cornish Ballads," p. 168.

2 M

I would not be forgotten in this land :
I yearn that men I know not, men unborn,
Should find, amid these fields, King Arthur's fame !
Here let them say, by proud Dundagel's walls—
" They brought the Sangraal back by his command,
They touched these rugged rocks with hues of God."
So shall my name have worship, and my land.[1]

[1] " Cornish Ballads," p. 186.

BIBLIOGRAPHY.

R. S. HAWKER.

WORKS.

[As a full bibliography of Hawker's books, leaflets, and contributions to magazines is included in the biography by Mr. C. E. Byles, to which reference is made below, only the latest editions are given here.]

Footprints of Former Men in Far Cornwall. (Complete Prose Works). Edited, with an introduction, by C. E. Byles. John Lane, 1903.

Cornish Ballads and Other Poems. (Complete Poetical Works with additional pieces previously unpublished.) Edited with an Introduction, by C. E. Byles. John Lane, 1904. Re-printed, 1908.

Stones Broken from the Rocks. (Extracts from the MS. Note-books . . . selected and arranged by E. R. Appleton.) Edited with a Preface, by C. E. Byles. Blackwell, 1922.

Twenty Poems. With an Introduction by John Drinkwater. Blackwell, 1925.

BIOGRAPHY.

Baring-Gould, Rev. S., *The Vicar of Morwenstow.* H. S. King & Co., 1876. 7th edition. Methuen, 1919.

Lee, Dr. F. G. *Memorials of the late R. S. Hawker.* Chatto & Windus, 1876.

Byles, C. E. *The Life and Letters of R. S. Hawker.* John Lane, 1905.

GENERAL.

LITERATURE.

Cambridge History of English Literature. Vols. VII., IX., XII., XIII.

Courthope, W. J. *History of English Poetry.* 6 vols. Macmillan, 1910.

Saintsbury, G. E. B. *History of English Prosody.* 3 Vols. Macmillan, 1923.

Walker, Hugh. *The Literature of the Victorian Era.* Cambridge, 1910.

Gosse, Sir. E. W. *Jacobean Poets.* John Murray, 1894.
Seventeenth Century Studies. Kegan, Paul & Co., 1883.

Smith, D. Nichol. *Characters from the Histories and Memoirs of the Seventeenth Century.* Oxford, 1918.

Spurgeon, Caroline F. E. *Mysticism in English Literature.* Cambridge, 1913.

Nutt, Alfred. *Studies on the Legend of the Holy Grail.* Folklore Society, 1888.

RELIGION.

(a) *Dogmatic.*

Bigg, Charles. *The Christian Platonists of Alexandria.* Oxford, 1913.

Wicksteed, P. H. *Dante and Aquinas, being the substance of the Jowett lectures of 1911.* Dent, 1913.

Tulloch, John. *Rational Theology and Christian Philosophy in England in the Seventeenth Century.* Edinburgh, 1874.

Stephen, Sir Leslie. *History of English Thought in the Eighteenth Century.* 2 Vols. Smith, Elder & Co., 1902.

Church, R. W. *The Oxford Movement, Twelve Years, 1833–45.* Macmillan, 1891.

Ward, Wilfrid P. *The Oxford Movement.* Jack, 1913.

(b) *Mystical.*

Underhill, Evelyn. *Mysticism.* Methuen, 1911.
(This contains a valuable bibliography of mystical works.)

Inge, W. R. *Christian Mysticism.* Methuen, 1899.

Jones, R. M. *Studies in Mystical Religion.* Macmillan, 1909.

Hügel, Baron F. von. *The Mystical Element in Religion.* 2 Vols. Dent, 1909.

Vaughan, R. A. *Hours with the Mystics.* 2 Vols. London, 1880.

Gregory, Eleanor C. *A Little Book of Heavenly Wisdom.* Selections from some English prose mystics, with Introduction. Methuen, 1902.

SCIENCE.

Lodge, Sir O. J. *The Ether of Space.* Harper, 1909.
Ether and Reality. Hodder & Stoughton, 1925.

Einstein, Albert. *Sidelights on Relativity.* Translated by Jeffery and Perrett. Methuen, 1922.

Harrow, B. *From Newton to Einstein.* Constable, 1920.

BIBLIOGRAPHY.

INDIVIDUAL WRITERS.

(References to works are given only where there might be difficulty about editions.)

FOREIGN.

St. Francis of Assisi. *Life of St. Francis* by St. Bonaventura. English Translation. (Temple Classics) London, 1904.
Sabatier, P. *Vie de S. François d'Assise.* 22ème édition. Paris, 1899.
Translated by L. S. Houghton. London, 1901.
(See also Bibliography to *Mysticism,* E. Underhill).
St. Thomas Aquinas. *Summa Theologica.* Literally translated by Fathers of the English Dominican Province. 2nd Edition. Burns, Oates & Washbourne, 1922.
Gretser, Jacob. *Opera omnia.* 17 tom. Ratisbonae, 1734–41.
Boehme, Jacob. *Works* (incomplete). 4 Vols. 1764–81.
Reprints, ed. C. J. Barker, pub. J. Watkins, *Aurora.* 1914.
A High and Deep Searching-out of the Threefold Life of Man. 1909.
(See Bibliography to Chap. XII. of Cambridge History of English Literature, Vol. IX.)
Swedenborg, Emmanuel. *Works.* Published by the Swedenborg Society, London. *Selections, A Compendium of the Theological Writings,* ed. Warren, 1901.
Principia. Ed. Rendell & Tansley. 1912.

ENGLISH. *17th Century.*

Donne, John. *Poetical Works.* Ed. Grierson. 2 Vols. Oxford, 1912.
Herbert, George. *English Works* newly arranged and annotated by G. H. Palmer. 3 Vols. Houghton Mifflin & Co. 1905.
Vaughan, Henry. *Poems.* Ed. Chambers. 2 Vols. 1896.
Traherne, Thomas. *Poetical Works.* Ed. Dobell. 1903.
Centuries of Meditations. Ed. Dobell. 1908.
Poems of Felicity. Ed. Bell, Oxford, 1910,
More, Henry. *Complete Poems.* Ed. Grosart. 1878.
Life by R. Ward, 1710. Reprinted Theosophical Society. Ed. Howard, 1911.
Norris, John. *Collected Poems.* Fuller Worthies Library. 1871.
Crashaw, Richard. *Poems.* Ed. A. R. Waller. Cambridge, 1904.
Herrick, Robert. *Poetical Works,* ed. Moorman. Oxford, 1915.
Moorman, F. W. *A biographical and critical study.* Lane, 1910.
Taylor, Jeremy. *Life* by Sir E. W. Gosse. (English Men of Letters). 1904.

18th Century.

Law, William. *Works.* 9 Vols. 1753–76. Reprinted privately by G. Moreton, 1892–3.
Liberal and Mystical Writings of William Law. Ed. W. Scott Palmer. 1908.
    (*See* Bibliography to Chap. XII. of Cambridge History of English Literature, Vol. IX.)

Blake, William. *Works.* Ed. Ellis & Yeats. 3 Vols. Quaritch. 1893.
Berger, P. *William Blake, Mysticisme et poésie.* Paris, 1907.
Damon, S. Foster. *William Blake.* Constable, 1924.

19th Century.

Tennyson, Alfred. Nicholson, H. *Tennyson.* Constable, 1924.

Patmore, Coventry. Champneys, B. *Memoirs and Correspondence of Coventry Patmore.* 2 Vols. George Bell, 1901.
Burdett, O. H. *The Idea of Coventry Patmore.* H. Milford, 1921.

Rossetti, Christina. *Poems.* Ed. W. M. Rossetti. Macmillan, 1918.

Thompson, Francis. *Works.* Ed. W. Meynell. 3 Vols. Burns & Oates, 1913.

Keble John. Lock, Walter. *John Keble.* Methuen, 1893.
Wood, Hon. E. F. L. *John Keble.* Mowbray, 1909.

Newman, J. H. Ward, Wilfrid. *Life of John Henry Newman.* 2 Vols. Longmans, 1913.

Williams, Isaac. *Autobiography of Isaac Williams.* Ed. by Sir G. Prevost. Longmans, 1892.

INDEX.

PRINTED AT THE VINCENT WORKS, OXFORD.